CAMBRIDGE TRAVEL BOOKS

THE

NORTH-WEST AND NORTH-EAST

PASSAGES, 1576–1611

T0345976

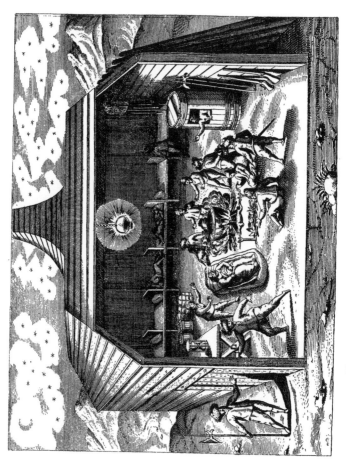

The exact manner of the house wherein we wintered

(Barents : Third Voyage)

THE

NORTH-WEST AND
NORTH-EAST PASSAGES
1576–1611

EDITED BY

PHILIP F. ALEXANDER, M.A.
HERTFORD COLLEGE, OXFORD

Cambridge :
at the University Press
1915

CAMBRIDGE UNIVERSITY PRESS
Cambridge, New York, Melbourne, Madrid, Cape Town,
Singapore, São Paulo, Delhi, Tokyo, Mexico City

Cambridge University Press
The Edinburgh Building, Cambridge CB2 8RU, UK

Published in the United States of America by
Cambridge University Press, New York

www.cambridge.org
Information on this title: www.cambridge.org/9781107600614

First published 1915
First paperback edition 2011

A catalogue record for this publication is available from the British Library

ISBN 978-1-107-60061-4 Paperback

PREFACE

THE aim of the present series is to illustrate the history of geographical discovery by means of select voyages and travels. These are usually written by the discoverer himself, or by an eye-witness who accompanied him on his journey. Apart from the results achieved, they are full of interest, since they tell the story of man's bravery in feeling his way over an unknown world.

The English voyages of the sixteenth century (some of which will be given in this series) record, moreover, the deeds of the seamen who laid the foundation of Britain's sea-power and of her Colonial Empire.

It is hoped that these books may be of service in schools, used either as Readers, or as an aid to the teaching of Geography. Spelling and punctuation have been modernized wherever necessary, though archaic words have been kept.

P. F. A.

WALBERSWICK,
May 1915.

CONTENTS

MAPS AND ILLUSTRATIONS

The only Passage (Bering Strait) and its approaches as known now

From Dr Bruce's Polar Exploration, by kind permission of Messrs Williams and Norgate)

INTRODUCTION

Venice, the seaport closest to the centre of Europe, had gradually pushed her trade farther and farther across the Mediterranean, until in the fifteenth century, after the crushing defeat of Genoa—her only serious rival—she was not only mistress of the Adriatic, but the commercial capital of the world. Her trade routes extended as far as the Sea of Azof, along the coasts of Asia Minor and Syria, and to Alexandria, whence her ships brought back the merchandise that had travelled from the East along the great caravan routes that stretched either from Suez to Alexandria, or from Ormuz (at the entrance of the Persian Gulf), to Beyrout or Aleppo. With this merchandise and the produce of the Mediterranean she traded by land with central Europe, and by sea to the west as far as England and Flanders. Her splendour is thus described by the poet Petrarch : " From my windows on the Riva degli Schiavoni, I see vessels as large as my house with masts taller than its towers. They sail to all parts of the world, and brave a thousand dangers. They carry wine to England ; honey to the Scythians ; saffron, oil, linen to Assyria, Armenia, Persia and Arabia ; wood to Egypt and Greece ; they return laden with merchandise to be distributed all over Europe. Where the sea ends, their sailors quit the ships and travel on to trade with India and China ; they cross the Caucasus and the Ganges, and reach the Eastern Ocean[1]."

From early in the fifteenth century Portuguese sailors, inspired by their Prince Henry, had been trying to find a sea-route to India, and though progress was very slow, their ships gradually crept down the coast of Africa, until in 1486 Bartholomew Diaz rounded the Cape of Good Hope. This was a deadly blow to Venetian prosperity, as goods could be brought far more cheaply from the East by sea than by land, especially because exorbitant duties were exacted from the caravans by the Mohammedan rulers of Syria and Egypt. Ten years later Vasco da Gama sailed round the Cape, and reached Calicut on the west coast of India. The Portuguese then established themselves at Goa on the same coast, seized Ormuz (one of the centres of the trade with Venice), and in 1521 the Moluccas or Spice Islands, and for fifty years held the monopoly of trade with the East.

Christopher Columbus and his brother Bartholomew, natives of Genoa, had after many voyages settled in Portugal, about the year 1470. Ignorant of the existence of America and the Pacific Ocean, Columbus was convinced that a much nearer route to China and India could be found by sailing westwards. As the Portuguese king would not grant him the assistance he needed for the voyage, he went to Spain and after years of waiting obtained all he asked from Ferdinand and Isabella. In 1492 he set sail and discovered islands lying as he supposed off the coast of Asia, and still known as the West Indies (the Indies reached by

---

[1] Quoted from *The Venetian Republic* by Horatio Brown (J. M. Dent and Co.).

the westward route). In 1493 the Pope, Alexander VI, issued a Bull which practically divided all the world outside Europe between Spain and Portugal, and then followed the gradual discovery of the American continent by Spanish and Portuguese fleets, the conquest of Mexico and Peru by the Spaniards, and the voyage of Magellan's ship the *Victoria* (the first voyage round the world) across the Pacific, by way of South America, proving the existence of another great ocean besides the Atlantic which lay between Europe and the East.

Other nations determined to obtain a share of the wealth that was pouring into Spain and Portugal from their new colonies. The French established themselves in Canada, and the English and Dutch made attempts to discover a way to the East, either by rounding the coast of North America, which tapered, it was believed, to a cape like Africa and South America (*The North-West Passage*), or by sailing round Norway and along the coasts of Russia and Siberia (*The North-East Passage*).

In the reign of Henry VII, another Genoese, John Cabot, who had settled in Bristol, had tried the north-west route, and had re-discovered Newfoundland and explored part of the coast of North America. In 1553 Sir Hugh Willoughby was lost in attempting the North-East Passage, but Richard Chancellor, his pilot, reached Archangel in another ship, and travelled overland to Moscow, opening a trade between England and Russia. For a time, owing to the success of this trade, no further attempt was made towards the north-east, and attention was again directed to the north-west.

In 1576 Martin Frobisher started on his first voyage, and discovered the passage into Baffin Land, now known as Frobisher Bay. In his two subsequent voyages, practically nothing was done in the way of discovery. They were indeed scarcely intended for anything more than a mining adventure.

John Davis, a Devonshire man, a friend of the Gilberts and their half-brother Sir Walter Ralegh, and one of the most capable navigators of Queen Elizabeth's reign, accomplished far more than any of his predecessors in the way of discovery during his three voyages of 1585–7. But his failure to find a passage led to renewed attempts on the part of the Dutch as well as the English towards the north and north-east, though already one important expedition, under Pet and Jackman, had been sent out in 1580 in the latter direction by the Russia or Muscovy Company, and had been driven back by the ice in the Kara Sea, with the loss of Jackman and his ship on the return journey.

In 1594 the Dutch, who had before made several attempts in the same direction, sent out three ships accompanied by a small fishing boat, two of them to follow the previous route by the south of Novaya Zemlya, and one, of which Barents was commander, together with the small boat, to attempt a passage round the north of the island. After reaching, with enormous difficulty, the Orange Islands, he was obliged to turn back, falling in on his return journey with the other ships which had been unable to cross the Kara Sea. The following year a larger expedition, with Barents as chief pilot, had no more success. In spite of this, two ships again set out next year, 1596, carrying Barents as pilot. They discovered Spitzbergen, and separated. Barents's ship (commanded by Heemskerck) then sailed for Novaya Zemlya, and after rounding the north of the island, was ice-bound on the east coast. Here the crew built a house and remained for ten months, in the hope that the ice would break up. Summer came, and as the ship was still fast, they embarked in two open boats, and after a voyage of nearly 1700 miles reached Kola, and found Dutch ships there, one of which took them back to Holland. Barents and four others had died, but twelve out of the ship's company of seventeen reached home in safety.

This voyage, told in vivid detail by De Veer, who accompanied Barents, is a very memorable one. For the first time on record men had wintered far within the Arctic zone. It had too a romantic sequel, when nearly 300 years afterwards the relics of the winter house were discovered. Barents is " perhaps the most hardy and capable navigator ever produced by Holland[1]."

To return to English attempts. Hudson in 1607 tried a new route to the north across the Polar Sea, and again next year the old route to the north-east by Novaya Zemlya. In 1609 he was employed by the Dutch East India Company, and after a vain attempt to pass Novaya Zemlya, he sailed westwards and explored part of the American coast, and the river which now bears his name, and on which New York stands. In 1610, at the expense of some London merchants, he set out on his last voyage, to attempt the North-West Passage. Sailing up the strait and into the bay, which are now named after him, he was

---

[1] Heawood, *A History of Geographical Discovery in the* 17*th and* 18*th centuries* (Cambridge University Press).

abandoned by his mutinous crew, and nothing more was ever heard of him.

In 1616, after several previous voyages, Baffin made considerable discoveries in the bay which bears his name. The attention of both English and Dutch was, however, turning to the whale fishery, which the voyages of Barents and Hudson had opened up, and little was done in the way of exploration for many years. It was not until 1728, when Peter the Great sent out Bering for this purpose, that it was actually proved that Asia was separated from America. He did not, however, attempt the North-East Passage, but sailed north from Kamtchatka, where he had built two ships. In a subsequent voyage (1741) he proved that the water that separated the two continents was a narrow strait. Early voyages had been mainly for commercial reasons, but Bering's were conducted in the cause of science. Of later expeditions in the same cause, the most famous are those of Sir John Franklin between 1819 and 1847, but it was not until 1850–54 that M'Clure accomplished the North-West Passage, nor until 1878–79 that a Swedish explorer, Nordenskiöld, succeeded in the North-East Passage, along the north coast of Siberia.

NOTE. Frobisher's and Davis's Voyages are taken from Hakluyt's *Principal Navigations, etc.* and are given nearly complete. Prickett's Narrative of Hudson's Last Voyage is from Purchas's *Pilgrims*, omitting the earlier and less interesting portion. Barents's Third Voyage is from a translation by W. Phillip published in 1609. I have abridged this considerably, and have used for the purpose, with the kind permission of the Hakluyt Society, the 2nd edition of *De Veer* issued by them in 1876. This contains many valuable corrections to Phillip's translation, a few of which I have incorporated in the text, while others will be found in the notes. The extracts from Carlsen's log-book are from the same source.

SOME IMPORTANT DATES IN THE
HISTORY OF DISCOVERY

B.C.

327. Alexander the Great reaches India.

55. Julius Caesar visits Britain.

A.D.

861. The Vikings (under Naddod) discover Iceland.

877. Gunnbiorn discovers Greenland, which is colonised a few years later by Eric the Red.

1000. Leif Ericson discovers Labrador (Helluland), Newfoundland (Markland) and Nova Scotia (Vinland). Colonies are founded, but afterwards abandoned.

1260–1271. Niccolo and Maffeo Polo (Marco Polo's father and uncle) go on a trading expedition through Asia to China.

1271–1295. Marco Polo goes with them on a second journey to the Court of Kublai Khan, and thence is sent as an envoy to Cochin China, India, etc.

1418–1460. Prince Henry of Portugal (Henry the Navigator) encourages discovery.

1420. Zarco discovers Madeira.

1455. Cadamosto reaches the Senegal and Cape Verde.

1484. Diego Cam discovers the Congo.

1486. Bartholomew Diaz rounds the Cape of Good Hope.

1492. Columbus discovers the West Indies.

1493. Columbus (2nd voyage) discovers Jamaica.

1497. Vasco da Gama reaches India by the Cape. On the way he sees Natal (Christmas Day), and Mozambique, and lands at Zanzibar.

1497. John Cabot re-discovers Newfoundland.

1498. Columbus (3rd voyage) discovers Trinidad and the Orinoco.

1499. Amerigo Vespucci discovers Venezuela (though great doubt is now cast on the accuracy of his statements).

1500. Pedro Cabral discovers Brazil.

1511. Serrano reaches the Moluccas (the Spice Islands).

1513. Balboa crosses the Isthmus of Panama, and sees the Pacific.

1519. Cortez conquers Mexico.

1519. Magellan starts on the first voyage round the world.

1520. Magellan sails past Monte Video, Patagonia, and Tierra del Fuego, through his strait, and across the Pacific.

1521. Magellan discovers the Ladrones, and is killed on the Philippines.

1522. Sebastian del Cano, in Magellan's ship, *Victoria*, reaches Spain.

1531. Pizarro conquers Peru.

1534. Cartier explores the St Lawrence.

1541. Orellana explores the Amazon.

1553. Sir Hugh Willoughby attempts the North-East Passage, and sees Novaya Zemlya.

1554. Chancellor, Willoughby's pilot, reaches Archangel, and travels thence to Moscow.

1558. Jenkinson travels from Moscow to Bokhara.

1576. Martin Frobisher discovers his bay.

1577–1580. Drake sails round the world—the first Englishman who does this.

1586–88. Cavendish sails round the world.

1586. Davis sails through his strait.

1596. Barents discovers Spitzbergen.

1605. Torres discovers his strait.

1608. Champlain discovers Lake Ontario.

1610. Hudson sails through his strait into his bay.

1615. Lemaire rounds Cape Horn (Hoorn, named after the town to which his ships belonged).

1616. Baffin discovers his bay.

1642. Tasman‑ discovers Van Diemen's Land (Tasmania) and Staaten Land (New Zealand).

1699. Dampier discovers his strait.

1768–71. Cook (1st voyage) discovers New Zealand and east coast of New Holland (Australia).

1770. Bruce discovers the source of the Blue Nile.

1776–79. Cook (3rd voyage) discovers the Sandwich Islands.

1785–88. La Pérouse explores N.E. coasts of Asia, the China and Japan Seas, and discovers Saghalien.

1789–93. Mackenzie discovers his river and British Columbia.
1792. Vancouver explores his island.
1796. Mungo Park reaches the Niger.
1797. Bass discovers his strait.
1799–1804. Humboldt explores South America.
1801–4. Flinders surveys the south coast of Australia.
1819–22. Franklin, Back and Richardson attempt the North-West Passage by land.
1819. Parry discovers Lancaster Sound.
1822. Denham and Clapperton discover Lake Tchad.
1828–31. Sturt traces the Darling and Murray Rivers.
1829–33. Ross attempts the North-West Passage, and discovers Boothia.
1840–42. Ross explores the Antarctic, and discovers Victoria Land, and the volcanoes Erebus and Terror (named after his ships).
1845–47. Franklin's last voyage.
1849–56. Livingstone explores the Zambesi, and discovers the Victoria Falls.
1850–54. M'Clure succeeds in the North-West Passage.
1858. Burton and Speke discover Lake Tanganyika, and Speke discovers Victoria Nyanza.
1858–62. Stuart crosses Australia from south to north.
1858–64. Livingstone explores Lake Nyasa.
1864. Baker. discovers Albert Nyanza.
1873. Livingstone discovers Lake Moero.
1874–5. Cameron crosses equatorial Africa.
1876–7. Stanley explores the Congo River, and opens up Centra Africa.
1878–79. Nordenskiöld succeeds in the North-East Passage.
1887–89. Stanley's expedition to rescue Emin Pasha. He discovers the Pigmies, and the Ruwenzori (the Mountains of the Moon).
1893–97. Nansen's voyage across the Arctic Ocean in the *Fram*. He reaches farthest north (86° 14′).
1909. Peary reaches the North Pole.
1911. Amundsen reaches the South Pole.
1912. Scott reaches the South Pole.

Sir Martin Frobisher

FROBISHER. FIRST VOYAGE (1576)

By George Best

Our General, Captain Frobisher, being persuaded of
a new and nearer passage to Cataya than by Capo
de Buona Sperança, which the Portugals yearly use,
began first with himself to devise, and then with his
friends to confer, and laid a plain plot unto them that
that voyage was not only possible by the north-west,
but also he could prove easy to be performed. And
further, he determined and resolved with himself to go
make full proof thereof, and to accomplish or bring
true certificate of the truth, or else never to return
again, knowing this to be the only thing of the world
that was left yet undone, whereby a notable mind might
be made famous and fortunate. But although his will
were great to perform this notable voyage, whereof he
had conceived in his mind a great hope by sundry sure
reasons and secret intelligence, which here for sundry
causes I leave untouched; yet he wanted altogether
means and ability to set forward, and perform the
same. Long time he conferred with his private friends
of these secrets, and made also many offers for the
performing of the same in effect unto sundry merchants
of our country, above fifteen years before he attempted
the same, as by good witness shall well appear (albeit
some evil willers, which challenge to themselves the fruits
of other men's labours, have greatly injured him in the

reports of the same, saying that they have been the
first authors of that action, and that they have learned
him the way, which themselves as yet have never gone).
But perceiving that hardly he was hearkened unto of
the merchants, which never regard virtue without sure,
certain, and present gains, he repaired to the Court
(from whence, as from the fountain of our common
wealth, all good causes have their chief increase and
maintenance), and there laid open to many great
estates and learned men the plot and sum of his device.
And amongst many honourable minds which favoured
his honest and commendable enterprise, he was specially
bound and beholding to the Right Honourable Ambrose
Dudley, Earl of Warwick, whose favourable mind and
good disposition hath always been ready to countenance
and advance all honest actions with the authors and
executers of the same.   And so by means of my lord
his honourable countenance he received some comfort
of his cause, and by little and little, with no small expense
and pain, brought his cause to some perfection, and
had drawn together so many adventurers and such sums
of money as might well defray a reasonable charge to
furnish himself to sea withal.

He prepared two small barks of twenty and five-and-
twenty ton apiece, wherein he intended to accomplish
his pretended voyage.   Wherefore, being furnished with
the foresaid two barks, and one small pinnace of ten ton
burthen, having therein victuals and other necessaries
for twelve months' provision, he departed upon the said
voyage from Blackwall, the 15 of June, anno Domini
1576.

One of the barks wherein he went was named
the *Gabriel*, and the other the *Michael* ; and sailing

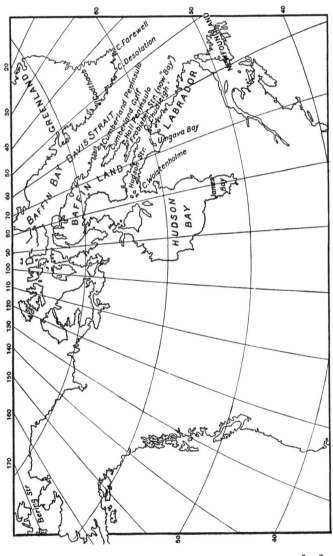

Part of North America and Greenland, to illustrate Frobisher's, Davis's, and Hudson's Voyages

north-west from England upon the 11 of July he had sight of a high and ragged land, which he judged to be Frisland (whereof some authors have made mention), but durst not approach the same by reason of the great store of ice that lay alongst the coast, and the great mists that troubled them not a little. Not far from thence he lost company of his small pinnace, which by means of the great storm he supposed to be swallowed up of the sea, wherein he lost only four men.

Also the other bark named the *Michael*, mistrusting the matter, conveyed themselves privily away from him, and returned home, with great report that he was cast away.

The worthy captain, notwithstanding these discomforts, although his mast was sprung, and his topmast blown overboard with extreme foul weather, continued his course towards the north-west, knowing that the sea at length must needs have an ending, and that some land should have a beginning that way; and determined, therefore, at the least to bring true proof what land and sea the same might be so far to the north-westwards, beyond any man that hath heretofore discovered. And the 20 of July he had sight of a high land which he called Queen Elizabeth's Foreland, after her Majesty's name. And sailing more northerly alongst that coast, he descried another foreland with a great gut, bay, or passage, dividing as it were two main lands or continents asunder. There he met with store of exceeding great ice all this coast along, and coveting still to continue his course to the northwards, was always by contrary wind detained overthwart these straits, and could not get beyond. Within few days after, he perceived the ice to be well consumed

and gone, either there engulfed in by some swift currents
or indrafts, carried more to the southwards of the same
straits, or else conveyed some other way : wherefore
he determined to make proof of this place, to see how
far that gut had continuance, and whether he might
carry himself through the same, into some open sea on
the back side, whereof he conceived no small hope, and
so entered the same, the one and twentieth of July, and
passed above fifty leagues therein, as he reported, having
upon either hand a great main or continent.   And that
land upon his right hand as he sailed westward he judged
to be the continent of Asia, and there to be divided
from the firm of America, which lieth upon the left
hand over against the same.

This place he named after his name, Frobisher's
Straits, like as Magellanus at the south-west end of the
world, having discovered the passage to the South Sea,
(where America is divided from the continent of that
land, which lieth under the South Pole) and called the
same straits, Magellan's Straits.

After he had passed 60 leagues into this foresaid
strait, he went ashore, and found signs where fire
had been made.

He saw mighty deer that seemed to be mankind,
which ran at him, and hardly he escaped with his life
in a narrow way, where he was fain to use defence
and policy to save his life.

In this place he saw and perceived sundry tokens
of the peoples resorting thither.   And being ashore upon
the top of a hill, he perceived a number of small things
fleeting in the sea afar off, which he supposed to be
porpoises or seals, or some kind of strange fish ; but
coming nearer, he discovered them to be men in small

boats made of leather.   And before he could descend
down from the hill, certain of those people had almost
cut off his boat from him, having stolen secretly behind
the rocks for that purpose, where he speedily hasted
to his boat, and bent himself to his halberd, and
narrowly escaped the danger, and saved his boat.
Afterwards he had sundry conferences with them, and
they came aboard his ship, and brought him salmon
and raw flesh and fish, and greedily devoured the same
before our men's faces.   And to shew their agility,
they tried many masteries upon the ropes of the ship,
after our mariners' fashion, and appeared to be very
strong of their arms, and nimble of their bodies.   They
exchanged coats of seals' and bears' skins, and such like,
with our men ; and received bells, looking-glasses, and
other toys, in recompense thereof again.   After great
courtesy, and many meetings, our mariners, contrary
to their captain's direction, began more easily to trust
them ; and five of our men going ashore were by them
intercepted with their boat, and were never since heard
of to this day again ; so that the captain being destitute
of boat, bark, and all company, had scarcely sufficient
number to conduct back his bark again.   He could now
neither convey himself ashore to rescue his men (if he
had been able) for want of a boat; and again the subtle
traitors were so wary, as they would after that never
come within our men's danger.   The captain, notwithstanding, desirous to bring some token from thence of
his being there, was greatly discontented that he had
not before apprehended some of them ; and therefore,
to deceive the deceivers, he wrought a pretty policy.
For knowing well how they greatly delighted in our toys,
and specially in bells, he rang a pretty lowbell, making

signs that he would give him the same that would come and fetch it. And because they would not come within his danger for fear, he flung one bell unto them, which of purpose he threw short, that it might fall into the sea and be lost. And to make them more greedy of the matter he rang a louder bell, so that in the end one of them came near the ship side to receive the bell. Which when he thought to take at the captain's hand, he was thereby taken himself; for the captain, being readily provided, let the bell fall, and caught the man fast, and plucked him with main force, boat and all, into his bark out of the sea. Whereupon, when he found himself in captivity, for very choler and disdain he bit his tongue in twain within his mouth: notwithstanding, he died not thereof, but lived until he came in England, and then he died of cold which he had taken at sea.

Now with this new prey (which was a sufficient witness of the captain's far and tedious travel towards the unknown parts of the world, as did well appear by this strange infidel, whose like was never seen, read, nor heard of before, and whose language was neither known nor understood of any) the said Captain Frobisher returned homeward, and arrived in England, in Harwich, the 2 of October following, and thence came to London 1576, where he was highly commended of all men for his great and notable attempt, but specially famous for the great hope he brought of the passage to Cataya.

And it is especially to be remembered that at their first arrival in those parts there lay so great store of ice all the coast along, so thick together, that hardly his boat could pass unto the shore. At length, after divers attempts, he commanded his company, if by any possible means they could get ashore, to bring him whatsoever thing they could first find, whether it were living or dead, stock or stone, in token of Christian possession, which thereby he took in behalf of the Queen's Most Excellent Majesty, thinking that thereby he might justify the having and enjoying of the same things that grew in these unknown parts.

Some of his company brought flowers, some green grass; and one brought a piece of black stone much like to a sea coal in colour, which by the weight seemed to be some kind of metal or mineral. This was a thing of no account in the judgment of the captain at the first sight; and yet for novelty it was kept in respect of the place from whence it came.

After his arrival in London, being demanded of sundry his friends what thing he had brought them home out of that country, he had nothing left to present them withal, but a piece of this black stone. And it fortuned a gentlewoman, one of the adventurers' wives, to have a piece thereof, which by chance she threw and burned in the fire, so long, that at the length being taken forth, and quenched in a little vinegar, it glistered with a bright marquesite of gold. Whereupon, the matter being called in some question, it was brought to certain goldfiners in London, to make assay thereof, who gave out that it held gold, and that very richly for the quantity. Afterwards the same goldfiners promised great matters thereof, if there were any store to be found, and offered themselves to adventure for the searching of those parts from whence the same was brought. Some that had great hope of the matter sought secretly to have a lease at Her Majesty's hands of those places, whereby to enjoy the mass of so great a public profit unto their own private gains.

In conclusion, the hope of more of the same gold ore to be found kindled a greater opinion in the hearts of many to advance the voyage again. Whereupon preparation was made for a new voyage against the year following, and the captain more specially directed by commission for the searching more of this gold ore than for the searching any further discovery of the passage. And being well accompanied with divers resolute and forward gentlemen, Her Majesty then lying at the Right Honourable the Lord of Warwick's house in Essex, he came to take his leave, and kissing Her Highness' hands, with gracious countenance and comfortable words departed toward his charge.

FROBISHER. SECOND VOYAGE

By His Lieutenant, George Best

A true report of such things as happened in the
second voyage of Captain Frobisher, pretended for
the discovery of a new passage to Cataya, China,
and the East India, by the north-west. Ann. Dom.
1577.

Being furnished with one tall ship of Her Majesty's,
named the *Aid*, of 200 ton, and two other small barks,
the one named the *Gabriel*, the other the *Michael*,
about 30 ton apiece, being fitly appointed with men,
munition, victuals and all things necessary for the
voyage, the said Captain Frobisher, with the rest of
his company, came aboard his ships riding at Blackwall,
intending (with God's help) to take the first wind and
tide serving him, the 25 day of May, in the year of
our Lord God 1577.

The names of such gentlemen as attempted this
discovery, and the number of soldiers and mariners in
each ship, as followeth.

Aboard the *Aid*, being Admiral, were the number of
100 men of all sorts, whereof 30 or more were gentlemen
and soldiers, the rest sufficient and tall sailors.

Aboard the *Gabriel*, being Vice-admiral, were in all
18 persons, whereof six were soldiers, the rest mariners.

Aboard the *Michael* were 16 persons, whereof five were soldiers, the rest mariners.

	General of the whole company for her Majesty	Martin Frobisher
	His Lieutenant	George Best
	His Ensign	Richard Philpot
	Corporal of the shot	Francis Forder
Aboard the *Aid* was		Henry Carew
		Edmund Stafford
		John Lee
	The rest of the gentlemen	M. Harvie
		Mathew Kinersley
		Abraham Lins
		Robert Kinersley
		Francis Brakenbury
		William Armshow
Aboard the *Aid* was	The Master	Christopher Hall
	The Mate	Charles Jackman
	The Pilot	Andrew Dyer
	The Master Gunner	Richard Cox
Aboard the *Gabriel* was	Captain	Edward Fenton
	One Gentleman	William Tamfield
	The Master	William Smith
Aboard the *Michael* was	Captain	Gilbert Yorke
	One Gentleman	Thomas Chamberlaine
	The Master	James Beare

On Whitsunday, being the 26 of May, Anno 1577, early in the morning, we weighed anchor at Blackwall, and fell that tide down to Gravesend, where we remained until Monday at night.

On Monday morning, the 27 of May, aboard the *Aid*, we received all the communion by the minister of Gravesend, and prepared us as good Christians towards God, and resolute men for all fortunes ; and towards night we departed to Tilbury Hope.

Tuesday, the 28 of May, about nine of the clock at night, we arrived at Harwich, in Essex, and there stayed for the taking in of certain victuals until Friday, being the 30th of May, during which time came letters from the Lords of the Council, straightly commanding our General not to exceed his complement and number appointed him, which was one hundred and twenty persons.   Whereupon he discharged many proper men, which with unwilling minds departed.

He also dismissed all his condemned men, which he thought for some purposes very needful for the voyage, and towards night upon Friday the one and thirtieth of May we set sail, and put to the seas again.   And sailing northward alongst the East coasts of England and Scotland, the 7th day of June we arrived in Saint Magnus Sound, in Orkney Islands, called in Latin Orcades, and came to anchor on the south side of the bay ; and this place is reckoned from Blackwall, where we set sail first, [cipher] leagues.

Here, our company going on land, the inhabitants of these islands began to flee as from the enemy.   Whereupon the lieutenant willed every man to stay together, and went himself unto their houses to declare what we were and the cause of our coming thither.   Which being understood, after their poor manner they friendly entreated us, and brought us for our money such things as they had.   And here our goldfiners found a mine of silver.

Orkney is the principal of the Isles of the Orcades, and standeth in the latitude of fifty-nine degrees and a half.   The country is much subject to cold, answerable for such a climate, and yet yieldeth some fruits, and sufficient maintenance for the people contented so poorly to live. There is plenty enough of poultry, store of eggs, fish, and fowl. For their bread they have oaten cakes, and their drink is ewes' milk, and in some parts ale. Their houses are but poor without and sluttish enough within, and the people in nature thereunto agreeable. For their fire they burn heath and turf, the country in most parts being void of wood. They have great want of leather, and desire our old shoes, apparel, and old ropes (before money) for their victuals, and yet are they not ignorant of the value of our coin. The chief town is called Kyrway. In this island hath been sometime an abbey or a religious house, called Saint Magnus, being on the west side of the isle, whereof this sound beareth name, through which we passed. Their governor or chief lord is called the Lord Robert Steward, who at our being there, as we understood, was in durance at Edinburgh, by the Regent's commandment of Scotland.

After we had provided us here of matter sufficient for our voyage, the 8 of June we set sail again, and passing through Saint Magnus Sound, having a merry wind by night, came clear and lost sight of all the land, and keeping our course west-north-west by the space of two days, the wind shifted upon us, so that we lay in traverse on the seas, with contrary winds, making good (as near as we could) our course to the westward, and sometime to the northward, as the wind shifted. And hereabout we met with three sail of English fishermen from Iceland, bound homeward, by whom we wrote our letters unto our friends in England. We traversed these seas by the space of 26 days without sight of any land, and met with much drift-wood, and whole bodies of trees. We saw many

monstrous fishes and strange fowls, which seemed to live
only by the sea, being there so far distant from any
land.   At length God favoured us with more prosperous
winds, and after we had sailed four days with good
wind in the poop, the 4th of July, the *Michael*,
being foremost ahead, shot off a piece of ordnance,
and struck all her sails, supposing that they descried
land, which by reason of the thick mists they could
not make perfect.   Howbeit, as well our account, as
also the great alteration of the water, which became
more black and smooth, did plainly declare we were
not far off the coast.   Our General sent his master
aboard the *Michael* (who had been with him the year
before) to bear in with the place to make proof thereof ;
who descried not the land perfect, but saw sundry huge
islands of ice, which we deemed to be not past twelve
leagues from the shore, for about ten of the clock at night,
being the fourth of July, the weather being more clear,
we made the land perfect, and knew it to be Frisland.
And the height being taken here, we found ourselves
to be in the latitude of sixty degrees and a half, and
were fallen with the southermost part of this land.
Between Orkney and Frisland are reckoned [cipher]
leagues.

This Frisland sheweth a ragged and high land,
having the mountains almost covered over with snow,
alongst the coast full of drift ice, and seemeth almost
inaccessible ; and is thought to be an island in bigness
not inferior to England, and is called of some authors,
West Frisland, I think because it lieth more west than
any part of Europe.   It extendeth in latitude to the
northward very far as seemed to us, and appeareth by
a description set out by two brethren Venetians,

Nicholas and Antonius Zeni, who, being driven off from Ireland with a violent tempest, made shipwreck here, and were the first known Christians that discovered this land, about 200 years sithence ; and they have in their sea-cards set out every part thereof, and described the condition of the inhabitants, declaring them to be as civil and religious people as we. And for so much of this land as we have sailed alongst, comparing their card with the coast, we find it very agreeable. This coast seemeth to have good fishing : for we, lying becalmed, let fall a hook without any bait, and presently caught a great fish called a halibut, which served the whole company for a day's meat, and is dangerous meat for surfeiting. And sounding about five leagues off from the shore, our lead brought up in the tallow a kind of coral, almost white, and small stones as bright as crystal : and it is not to be doubted but that this land may be found very rich and beneficial if it were thoroughly discovered, although we saw no creature there but little birds. It is a marvellous thing to behold of what great bigness and depth some islands of ice be here, some seventy, some eighty fathom under water, besides that which is above, seeming islands more than half a mile in circuit. All these ice are in taste fresh, and seem to be bred in the sounds thereabouts, or in some land near the pole, and with the wind and tides are driven alongst the coasts. We found none of these islands of ice salt in taste, whereby it appeareth that they were not congealed of the ocean sea-water, which is always salt, but of some standing or little-moving lakes, or great fresh waters near the shore, caused either by melted snow from tops of mountains, or by continual access of fresh rivers from the land ; and

intermingling with the sea-water, bearing yet the
dominion, by the force of extreme frost may cause
some part of salt water to freeze so with it, and so seem
a little brackish; but otherwise the main sea freezeth
not, and therefore there is no Mare Glaciale, or Frozen
Sea, as the opinion hitherto hath been. Our General
proved landing here twice, but by the sudden fall of mists
(whereunto this coast is much subject) he was like to
lose sight of his ships, and being greatly endangered
with the driving ice alongst the coast, was forced aboard,
and fain to surcease his pretence till a better opportunity
might serve. And having spent four days and nights
sailing alongst this land, finding the coast subject to
such bitter cold and continual mists, he determined
to spend no more time therein, but to bear out his
course towards the straits called Frobisher's Straits,
after the General's name, who being the first that ever
passed beyond 58 degrees to the northwards, for anything that hath been yet known of certainty, of Newfoundland, otherwise called the continent or firm land of
America, discovered the said Straits this last year 1576.

Between Frisland and the Straits we had one great
storm, wherein the *Michael* was somewhat in danger,
having her steerage broken, and her top-masts blown
overboard; and being not past 50 leagues short of the
Straits by our account, we struck sail and lay ahull,
fearing the continuance of the storm, the wind being
at the north-east, and having lost company of the barks
in that flaw of wind, we happily met again the 17th day
of July, having the evening before seen divers islands
of fleeting ice, which gave an argument that we were
not far from land. Our General, in the morning, from
the maintop (the weather being reasonable clear)

descried land; but to be better assured he sent the two barks two contrary courses, whereby they might descry either the south or north foreland, the *Aid* lying off and on at sea, with a small sail, by an island of ice, which was the mark for us to meet together again. And about noon, the weather being more clear, we made the north foreland perfect, which otherwise is called Hall's Island, and also the small island bearing the name of the said Hall, whence the ore was taken up which was brought into England this last year 1576, the said Hall being present at the finding and taking up thereof, who was then master in the *Gabriel* with Captain Frobisher. At our arrival here, all the seas about this coast were so covered over with huge quantity of great ice, that we thought these places might only deserve the name of Mare Glaciale, and be called the Icy Sea.

This north foreland is thought to be divided from the continent of the northerland, by a little sound called Hall's Sound, which maketh it an island, and is thought little less than the Isle of Wight, and is the first entrance of the straits upon the norther side, and standeth in the latitude of sixty-two degrees and fifty minutes, and is reckoned from Frisland [cipher] leagues. God having blessed us with so happy a land-fall, we bare into the straits, which run in next hand, and somewhat further up to the northward, and came as near the shore as we might for the ice; and upon the 18th day of July, our General, taking the goldfiners with him, attempted to go on shore with a small rowing pinnace, upon the small island where the ore was taken up, to prove whether there were any store thereof to be found, but he could not get in all that island a piece so big

as a walnut, where the first was found.   But our
men, which sought the other islands thereabouts, found
them all to have good store of the ore : whereupon our
General with these good tidings returned aboard about
ten of the clock at night, and was joyfully welcomed
of the company with a volley of shot.   He brought
eggs, fowls, and a young seal aboard, which the company
had killed ashore ; and having found upon those islands
gins set to catch fowl, and sticks new cut, with other
things, he well perceived that not long before some of
the country people had resorted thither.

Having therefore found those tokens of the people's
access in those parts, and being in his first voyage
well acquainted with their subtle and cruel disposition,
he provided well for his better safety ; and on Friday
the 19th of July, in the morning early, with his best
company of gentlemen and soldiers, to the number of
forty persons, went on shore, as well to discover the inland and habitation of the people, as also to find out some
fit harbour for our ships.   And passing towards the
shore with no small difficulty by reason of the abundance of ice, which lay alongst the coast so thick
together that hardly any passage through them might
be discovered, we arrived at length upon the main of
Hall's greater island, and found there also, as well as
in the other small islands, good store of the ore.   And
leaving his boats here with sufficient guard, we passed
up into the country about two English miles, and
recovered the top of a high hill ; on the top whereof
our men made a column or cross of stones heaped up
of a good height together in good sort, and solemnly
sounded a trumpet, and said certain prayers kneeling
about the ensign, and honoured the place by the name

of Mount Warwick, in remembrance of the Right
Honourable the Lord Ambrose Dudley, Earl of Warwick,
whose noble mind and good countenance in this, as in all
other good actions, gave great encouragement and good
furtherance. This done, we retired our companies, not
seeing anything here worth further discovery, the
country seeming barren and full of ragged mountains,
and in most parts covered with snow.

And thus marching towards our boats, we espied
certain of the country people on the top of Mount
Warwick with a flag wafting us back again and making
great noise, with cries like the mowing of bulls, seeming
greatly desirous of conference with us. Whereupon the
General, being therewith better acquainted, answered
them again with the like cries, whereat, and with the
noise of our trumpets, they seemed greatly to rejoice,
skipping, laughing and dancing for joy. And hereupon
we made signs unto them, holding up two fingers,
commanding two of our men to go apart from our
companies, whereby they might do the like. So that
forthwith two of our men and two of theirs met together
a good space from company, neither party having
their weapons about them. Our men gave them pins
and points and such trifles as they had. And they
likewise bestowed on our men two bow cases and such
things as they had. They earnestly desired our men
to go up into their country, and our men offered them
like kindness aboard our ships, but neither part (as it
seemed) admitted or trusted the other's courtesy.
Their manner of traffic is thus : they do use to lay down
of their merchandise upon the ground, so much as they
mean to part withal, and so looking that the other
party with whom they make trade should do the like,

they themselves do depart.   And then, if they do like
of their mart, they come again, and take in exchange
the other's merchandise : otherwise, if they like not, they
take their own and depart.   The day being thus well
near spent, in haste we retired our companies into our
boats again, minding forthwith to search alongst the
coast for some harbour fit for our ships.   For the present
necessity thereof was much, considering that all this
while they lay off and on between the two lands, being
continually subject as well to great danger of fleeting
ice, which environed them, as to the sudden flaws which
the coast seemeth much subject unto.   But when the
people perceived our departure, with great tokens of
affection they earnestly called us back again, following
us almost to our boats.   Whereupon our General, taking
his master with him, who was best acquainted with their
manners, went apart unto two of them, meaning, if they
could lay sure hold upon them, forcibly to bring them
aboard, with intent to bestow certain toys and apparel
upon the one, and so to dismiss him with all arguments
of courtesy, and retain the other for an interpreter.
The General and his master being met with their two
companions together, after they had exchanged certain
things the one with the other, one of the savages, for
lack of better merchandise, cut off the tail of his coat
(which is a chief ornament among them) and gave it
unto our General for a present.   But he presently, upon
a watchword given with his master, suddenly laid hold
upon the two savages.   But the ground underfoot being
slippery with the snow on the side of the hill, their
handfast failed, and their prey escaping ran away and
lightly recovered their bow and arrows, which they had
hid not far from them behind the rocks.   And being

only two savages in sight, they so fiercely, desperately, and with such fury assaulted and pursued our General and his master, being altogether unarmed, and not mistrusting their subtlety, that they chased them to their boats, and hurt the General in the buttock with an arrow; who the rather speedily fled back, because they suspected a greater number behind the rocks. Our soldiers (which were commanded before to keep their boats) perceiving the danger, and hearing our men calling for shot, came speedily to rescue, thinking there had been a greater number. But when the savages heard the shot of one of our calivers (and yet having first bestowed their arrows) they ran away, our men speedily following them. But a servant of my Lord of Warwick, called Nicholas Conger, a good footman, and uncumbered with any furniture, having only a dagger at his back, overtook one of them, and being a Cornish-man and a good wrestler, showed his companion such a Cornish trick, that he made his sides ache against the ground for a month after. And so being stayed, he was taken alive and brought away, but the other escaped. Thus with their strange and new prey our men repaired to their boats, and passed from the main to a small island of a mile compass, where they resolved to tarry all night; for even now a sudden storm was grown so great at sea, that by no means they could recover their ships. And here every man refreshed himself with a small portion of victuals, which was laid into the boats for their dinners, having neither eat nor drunk all the day before. But because they knew not how long the storm might last, nor how far off the ships might be put to sea, nor whether they should ever recover them again or not, they made great spare of their victuals, as it greatly behoved them. For they knew full well that the best cheer the country could yield them was rocks and stones, a hard food to live withal, and the people more ready to eat them than to give them wherewithal to eat. And thus keeping very good watch and ward, they lay there all night upon hard cliffs of snow and ice, both wet, cold, and comfortless.

These things thus happening with the company on land, the danger of the ships at sea was no less perilous. For within one hour after the General's departing in the morning, by negligence of the cook in over-heating, and the workman in making the chimney, the *Aid* was set on fire, and had been the confusion of the whole if, by chance a boy espying it, it had not been speedily with great labour and God's help well extinguished.

This day also were divers storms and flaws, and by nine of the clock at night the storm was grown so great, and continued such until the morning, that it put our ships at sea in no small peril. But God being our best steersman, and by the industry of Charles Jackman and Andrew Dyer, the master's mates, both very expert mariners, and Richard Cox, the master gunner, with other very careful sailors, then within board, and also by the help of the clear nights, which are without darkness, we did happily avoid those present dangers. Whereat since we have more marvelled than in the present danger feared; for that every man within board, both better and worse, had enough to do with his hands to haul ropes, and with his eyes to look out for danger. But the next morning, being the 20 of July, as God would, the storm ceased; and the General, espying the ships, with his new captive and whole company came happily aboard, and reported what had passed on shore. Whereupon all together upon our knees we gave God humble and hearty thanks, for that it had pleased Him from so speedy peril to send us such speedy deliverance. And so from this northern shore we struck over towards the souther-land.

The one and twentieth of July, we discovered a bay which ran into the land, that seemed a likely harbour for our ships. Wherefore our General rowed thither with his boats, to make proof thereof, and with his goldfiners to search for ore, having never assayed anything on the south shore as yet. And the first small island, which we landed upon, here all the sands and clifts did so glister and had so bright a marquesite, that it seemed all to be gold; but upon trial made, it proved no better than blacklead, and verified the proverb : All is not gold that glistereth.

Upon the two and twentieth of July we bare into the said sound, and came to anchor a reasonable breadth off the shore. And this was named Jackman's Sound, after the name of the master's mate, who had first liking unto the place.

Upon a small island, within this sound, called Smith's Island (because he first set up his forge there) was found a mine of silver, but was not won out of the rocks without great labour. Here our goldfiners made say of such ore as they found upon the norther-land, and found four sorts thereof to hold gold in good quantity. Upon another small island here was also found a great dead fish, which, as it should seem, had been embayed with ice, and was in proportion round like to a porpoise, being about twelve foot long, and in bigness answerable, having a horn of two yards long growing out of the snout or nostrils. This horn is wreathed and straight, like in fashion to a taper made of wax, and may truly be thought to be the sea-unicorn. This horn is to be seen and reserved as a jewel by the Queen's Majesty's commandment, in her wardrobe of robes.

Tuesday, the three and twentieth of July, our General with his best company of gentlemen, soldiers and sailors, to the number of seventy persons in all, marched with ensign displayed upon the continent of the southerland (the supposed continent of America). Where, commanding a trumpet to sound a call for every man to repair to the ensign, he declared to the whole company how much the cause imported for the service of Her Majesty, our country, our credits, and the safety of our own lives, and therefore required every man to be conformable to order, and to be directed by those he should assign.   And he appointed for leaders, Captain Fenton, Captain Yorke, and his Lieutenant, George Best. Which done, we cast ourselves into a ring, and all together upon our knees, gave God humble thanks for that it had pleased Him of His great goodness to preserve us from such imminent dangers ; beseeching likewise the assistance of His Holy Spirit, so to deliver us in safety into our country, whereby the light and truth of these secrets being known, it might redound to the more honour of His Holy Name, and consequently to the advancement of our common wealth.   And so, in as good sort as the place suffered, we marched towards the tops of the mountains, which were no less painful in climbing than dangerous in descending, by reason of their steepness and ice. And having passed about five miles, by such unwieldy ways, we returned unto our ships without sight of any people, or likelihood of habitation. Here divers of the gentlemen desired our General to suffer them, to the number of twenty or thirty persons, to march up thirty or forty leagues in the country, to the end they might discover the inland, and do some acceptable service for their country. But he, not contented with the matter he sought for, and well considering the short time he had in hand, and the greedy desire our country hath to a present savour and return of gain, bent his whole endeavour only to find a mine to freight his ships, and to leave the rest (by God's help) hereafter to be well accomplished. And therefore the twenty-six of July he departed over to the northland, with the two barks, leaving the *Aid* riding in Jackman's Sound, and meant (after he had found convenient harbour, and freight there for his ships) to discover further for the passage. The barks came the same night to anchor in a sound upon the northerland, where the tides did run so swift, and the place was so subject to indrafts of ice, that by reason thereof they were greatly endangered; and having found a very rich mine, as they supposed, and got almost twenty ton of ore together, upon the 28 of July the ice came driving into the sound where the barks rode, in such sort that they were therewith greatly distressed. And the *Gabriel*, riding astern the *Michael*, had her cable galled asunder in the hawse with a piece of driving ice, and lost another anchor; and having but one cable and anchor left, for she had lost two before, and the ice still driving upon her, she was (by God's help) well fenced from the danger

of the rest, by one great island of ice, which came
aground hard ahead of her. Which if it had not so
chanced, I think surely she had been cast upon the
rocks with the ice. The *Michael* moored anchor
upon this great ice, and rode under the lee thereof :
but about midnight, by the weight of itself, and
the setting of the tides, the ice brake within half the
bark's length, and made unto the company within
board a sudden and fearful noise. The next flood
toward the morning we weighed anchor, and went
further up the straits ; and leaving our ore behind
us which we had digged, for haste, left the place, by the
name of Beare's Sound, after the master's name of
the *Michael*, and named the island Leicester's Island.
In one of the small islands here we found a tomb,
wherein the bones of a dead man lay together, and
our savage captive being with us, and being demanded
by signs whether his countrymen had not slain this
man and eat his flesh so from the bones, he made
signs to the contrary, and that he was slain with wolves
and wild beasts. Here also was found hid under
stones good store of fish, and sundry other things
of the inhabitants ; as sleds, bridles, kettles of fish
skins, knives of bone, and such other like. And our
savage declared unto us the use of all those things.
And taking in his hand one of those country bridles,
he caught one of our dogs and hampered him handsomely
therein, as we do our horses, and with a whip in his hand,
he taught the dog to draw in a sled as we do horses
in a coach, setting himself thereupon like a guide :
so that we might see they use dogs for that purpose
that we do our horses. And we found since by experience, that the lesser sort of dogs they feed fat,

and keep them as domestical cattle in their tents for their eating, and the greater sort serve for the use of drawing their sleds.

The twenty-ninth of July, about five leagues from Beare's Sound, we discovered a bay which, being fenced on each side with small islands lying off the main, which break the force of the tides, and make the place free from any indrafts of ice, did prove a very fit harbour for our ships; where we came to anchor under a small island, which now together with the sound is called by the name of that right honourable and virtuous lady, Anne Countess of Warwick. And this is the furthest place that this year we have entered up within the straits, and is reckoned from the Cape of the Queen's Foreland, which is the entrance of the straits, not above 30 leagues. Upon this island was found good store of the ore, which in the washing held gold to our thinking plainly to be seen : whereupon it was thought best rather to load here, where there was store and indifferent good, than to seek further for better, and spend time with jeopardy. And therefore our General setting the miners to work, and shewing first a good precedent of a painful labourer and a good captain in himself, gave good examples for others to follow him : whereupon every man, both better and worse, with their best endeavours willingly laid to their helping hands. And the next day, being the thirtieth of July, the *Michael* was sent over to Jackman's Sound, for the *Aid* and the whole company to come thither. Upon the mainland, over against the Countess's Island, we discovered and beheld to our great marvel the poor caves and houses of those country people, which

serve them (as it should seem) for their winter dwellings,
and are made two fathom under ground, in compass
round, like to an oven, being joined fast one by another,
having holes like to a fox or cony bury, to keep
and come together.   They under-trenched these places
with gutters, so that the water, falling from the hills
above them, may slide away without their annoyance :
and are seated commonly in the foot of a hill, to
shield them better from the cold winds, having their
door and entrance ever open towards the south.   From
the ground upward they build with whales' bones,
for lack of timber, which bending one over another,
are handsomely compacted in the top together, and
are covered over with sealskins, which, instead of
tiles, fence them from the rain.   In which house
they have only one room, having the one half of the
floor raised with broad stones a foot higher than the
other, whereon strawing moss, they make their nests
to sleep in.   They defile these dens most filthily with
their beastly feeding, and dwell so long in a place
(as we think) until their sluttishness loathing them,
they are forced to seek a sweeter air, and a new seat ;
and are (no doubt) a dispersed and wandering nation,
as the Tartarians, and live in hoards and troops,
without any certain abode, as may appear by sundry
circumstances of our experience.

Here our captive being ashore with us, to declare
the use of such things as we saw, stayed himself
alone behind the company, and did set up five small
sticks round in a circle one by another, with one
small bone placed just in the midst of all : which
thing when one of our men perceived, he called us
back to behold the matter, thinking that he had meant

some charm or witchcraft therein. But the best
conjecture we could make thereof was, that he would
thereby his countrymen should understand, that for
our five men which they betrayed the last year (whom
he signified by the five sticks) he was taken and kept
prisoner, which he signified by the bone in the midst.
For afterwards when we shewed him the picture
of his countryman, which the last year was brought
into England (whose counterfeit we had drawn, with
boat and other furniture, both as he was in his own,
and also in English apparel), he was upon the sudden
much amazed thereat; and beholding advisedly the
same with silence a good while, as though he would
strain courtesy whether should begin the speech
(for he thought him no doubt a lively creature) at
length began to question with him, as with his companion; and finding him dumb and mute, seemed
to suspect him, as one disdainful, and would with
a little help have grown into choler at the matter,
until at last, by feeling and handling, he found him
but a deceiving picture. And then with great noise
and cries, ceased not wondering, thinking that we
could make men live or die at our pleasure. And
thereupon calling the matter to his remembrance,
he gave us plainly to understand by signs, that
he had knowledge of the taking of our five men the
last year, and confessing the manner of each thing,
numbered the five men upon his five fingers, and pointed
unto a boat in our ship, which was like unto that
wherein our men were betrayed : and when we made
him signs, that they were slain and eaten, he earnestly
denied, and made signs to the contrary.

The last of July the *Michael* returned with the

Aid to us from the southerland, and came to anchor
by us in the Countess of Warwick's Sound, and reported
that since we departed from Jackman's Sound there
happened nothing among them there greatly worth
the remembrance, until the thirtieth of July, when
certain of our company being ashore upon a small
island within the said Jackman's Sound, near the
place where the *Aid* rode, did espy a long boat with
divers of the country people therein, to the number
of eighteen or twenty persons. Whom so soon as our
men perceived, they returned speedily aboard, to
give notice thereof unto our company. They might
perceive these people climbing up to the top of a hill,
where, with a flag, they wafted unto our ship, and
made great outcries and noises, like so many bulls.
Hereupon our men did presently man forth a small
skiff, having not above six or seven persons therein,
which rowed near the place where those people
were, to prove if they could have any conference with
them. But after this small boat was sent a greater,
being well appointed for their rescue, if need required.
As soon as they espied our company coming near
them, they took their boats and hasted away, either for
fear, or else for policy, to draw our men from rescue
further within their danger : wherefore our men
construing that their coming thither was but to seek
advantage, followed speedily after them. But they
rowed so swiftly away that our men could come nothing
near them. Howbeit they failed not of their best
endeavour in rowing, and having chased them above
two miles into the sea, returned into their ships again.

The morning following, being the first of August,
Captain Yorke with the *Michael* came into Jackman's

Sound, and declared unto the company there, that the last night past he came to anchor in a certain bay (which sithence was named Yorke's Sound) about four leagues distant from Jackman's Sound, being put to leeward of that place for lack of wind, where he discovered certain tents of the country people; where going with his company ashore, he entered into them, but found the people departed, as it should seem, for fear of their coming. But amongst sundry strange things which in these tents they found, there was raw and new killed flesh of unknown sorts, with dead carcasses and bones of dogs, and I know not what. They also beheld (to their greatest marvel) a doublet of canvas made after the English fashion, a shirt, a girdle, three shoes for contrary feet, and of unequal bigness, which they well conjectured to be the apparel of our five poor countrymen, which were intercepted the last year by these country people, about fifty leagues from this place, further within the straits. Whereupon our men being in good hope that some of them might be here, and yet living, the captain, devising for the best, left his mind behind him in writing, with pen, ink, and paper also, whereby our poor captive countrymen, if it might come to their hands, might know their friends' minds, and of their arrival, and likewise return their answer. And so without taking anything away in their tents, leaving there also looking-glasses, points, and other of our toys (the better to allure them by such friendly means) departed aboard his bark, with intent to make haste to the *Aid*, to give notice unto the company of all such things as he had there discovered : and so meant to return to these tents again, hoping that he might by force

or policy entrap or entice the people to some friendly
conference. Which things when he had delivered
to the whole company there, they determined forthwith
to go in hand with the matter. Hereupon Captain
Yorke with the master of the *Aid*, and his mate (who
the night before had been at the tents, and came
over from the other side in the *Michael* with him),
being accompanied with the gentlemen and soldiers
to the number of thirty or forty persons, in two small
rowing pinnaces made towards the place, where the
night before they discovered the tents of those people,
and setting Charles Jackman, being the master's
mate, ashore with a convenient number, for that
he could best guide them to the place, they marched
over land, meaning to compass them on the one side,
whilst the captain with his boats might entrap them
on the other side. But landing at last at the place
where the night before they left them, they found
them with their tents removed. Notwithstanding,
our men which marched up into the country, passing
over two or three mountains, by chance espied certain
tents in a valley underneath them near unto a creek
by the seaside; which because it was not the place
where the guide had been the night before, they
judged them to be another company, and besetting
them about, determined to take them if they could.
But they, having quickly descried our company,
launched one great and another small boat, being
about sixteen or eighteen persons, and very narrowly
escaping, put themselves to sea. Whereupon our
soldiers discharged their calivers, and followed them,
thinking the noise thereof being heard to our boats
at sea, our men there would make what speed they

might to that place. And thereupon indeed our men which were in the boats (crossing upon them in the mouth of the sound, whereby their passage was let from getting sea room, wherein it had been impossible for us to overtake them by rowing,) forced them to put themselves ashore upon a point of land within the said sound (which upon the occasion of the slaughter there, was since named The Bloody Point). Whereunto our men so speedily followed, that they had little leisure left them to make any escape. But so soon as they landed, each of them brake his oar, thinking by that means to prevent us in carrying away their boats, for want of oars. And desperately returning upon our men, resisted them manfully in their landing, so long as their arrows and darts lasted; and after gathering up those arrows which our men shot at them, yea, and plucking our arrows out of their bodies, encountered afresh again, and maintained their cause until both weapons and life failed them. And when they found they were mortally wounded, being ignorant what mercy meaneth, with deadly fury they cast themselves headlong from off the rocks into the sea, lest perhaps their enemies should receive glory or prey of their dead carcasses, for they supposed us belike to be cannibals or eaters of man's flesh. In this conflict one of our men was dangerously hurt in the belly with one of their arrows, and of them were slain five or six, the rest by flight escaping among the rocks; saving two women, whereof the one being old and ugly, our men thought she had been a devil or some witch, and therefore let her go. The other, being young and cumbered with a sucking child at her back, hiding herself behind the rocks, was espied by one of our men, who supposing she had been a man, shot through the hair of her head, and pierced through the child's arm. Whereupon she cried out; and our surgeon meaning to heal her child's arm, applied salves thereunto. But she, not acquainted with such kind of surgery, plucked those salves away; and by continual licking with her own tongue, not much unlike our dogs, healed up the child's arm. And because the day was well near spent, our men made haste unto the rest of our company, which on the other side of the water remained at the tents; where they found by the apparel, letter, and other English furniture, that they were the same company which Captain Yorke discovered the night before, having removed themselves from the place where he left them.

And now, considering their sudden flying from our men, and their desperate manner of fighting, we began to suspect that we had heard the last news of our men, which the last year were betrayed of these people. And considering also their ravenous and bloody disposition in eating any kind of raw flesh or carrion, howsoever stinking, it is to be thought that they had slain and devoured our men : for the doublet which was found in their tents had many holes therein, being made with their arrows and darts.

But now the night being at hand, our men, with their captives and such poor stuff as they found in their tents, returned towards their ships. When, being at sea, there arose a sudden flaw of wind, which was not a little dangerous for their small boats; but, as God would, they came all safely aboard. And with these good news they returned (as before mentioned)

into the Countess of Warwick's Sound unto us. And
between Jackman's Sound, from whence they came,
and the Countess of Warwick's Sound, between land
and land, being thought the narrowest place of the
straits, were judged nine leagues over at the least:
and Jackman's Sound, being upon the southerland,
lieth directly almost over against the Countess's
Sound, as is reckoned scarce thirty leagues within
the straits from the Queen's Cape, which is the
entrance of the straits of the southerland. This cape
being named Queen Elizabeth's Cape, standeth in the
latitude of 62 degrees and a half to the northwards
of Newfoundland, and upon the same continent, for
anything that is yet known to the contrary.

Having now got a woman captive for the comfort
of our man, we brought them both together, and every
man with silence desired to behold the manner of
their meeting and entertainment, the which was
more worth the beholding than can be well expressed
by writing. At their first encountering they beheld
each the other very wistly a good space, without speech
or word uttered, with great change of colour and
countenance, as though it seemed the grief and disdain
of their captivity had taken away the use of their
tongues and utterance. The woman at the first very
suddenly, as though she disdained or regarded not
the man, turned away and began to sing, as though
she minded another matter : but being again brought
together, the man brake up the silence first, and with
stern and staid countenance, began to tell a long
solemn tale to the woman. Whereunto she gave good
hearing, and interrupted him nothing, till he had
finished ; and afterwards, being grown into more

familiar acquaintance by speech, they were turned
together, so that (I think) the one would hardly have
lived without the comfort of the other.

On Monday, the sixth of August, the lieutenant
with all the soldiers, for the better guard of the miners
and the other things ashore, pitched their tents in
the Countess's Island, and fortified the place for their
better defence as well as they could, and were to the
number of forty persons, when, being all at labour,
they might perceive upon the top of a hill over against
them a number of the country people wafting with
a flag, and making great outcries unto them, and were
of the same company which had encountered lately
our men upon the other shore, being come to complain
their late losses, and to entreat (as it seemed) for
restitution of the woman and child, which our men
in the late conflict had taken and brought away.
Whereupon the General, taking the savage captive
with him, and setting the woman where they might
best perceive her, in the highest place of the island,
went over to talk with them. This captive, at his
first encounter of his friends, fell so out into tears
that he could not speak a word in a great space; but
after a while, overcoming his kindness, he talked
at full with his companions, and bestowed friendly
upon them such toys and trifles as we had given him:
whereby we noted, that they are very kind one to
another, and greatly sorrowful for the loss of their
friends. Our General, by signs, required his five men
which they took captive the last year, and promised
them, not only to release those which he had taken,
but also to reward them with great gifts and friendship.
Our savage made signs in answer from them that

our men should be delivered us, and were yet living, and made signs likewise unto us that we should write our letters unto them. For they knew very well the use we have of writing, and received knowledge thereof, either of our poor captive countrymen which they betrayed, or else by this our new captive, who hath seen us daily write and repeat again such words of his language as we desired to learn. But they for this night, because it was late, departed without any letter, although they called earnestly in haste for the same. And the next morning early, being the seventh of August, they called again for the letter; which being delivered unto them, they speedily departed, making signs with three fingers, and pointing to the sun, that they meant to return within three days; until which time we heard no more of them; and about the time appointed they returned, in such sort as you shall afterwards hear.

This night, because the people were very near unto us, the lieutenant caused the trumpet to sound a call, and every man in the island repairing to the ensign, he put them in mind of the place, so far from their country wherein they lived, and the danger of a great multitude, which they were subject unto, if good watch and ward were not kept. For at every low water the enemy might come almost dryfoot from the main unto us; wherefore he willed every man to prepare him in good readiness upon all sudden occasions. And so, giving the watch their charge, the company departed to rest.

I thought the captain's letter well worth the remembering, not for the circumstance of curious inditing, but for the substance and good meaning therein contained, and therefore have repeated here the same, as by himself it was hastily written.

The form of Master Martin Frobisher's letter to the English captives.

'In the name of God, in whom we all believe, who (I trust) hath preserved your bodies and souls among these infidels, I commend me unto you. I will be glad to seek by all means you can devise for your deliverance, either with force, or with any commodities within my ships, which I will not spare for your sakes, or anything else I can do for you. I have aboard, of theirs, a man, a woman, and a child, which I am contented to deliver for you, but the man which I carried away from hence the last year is dead in England. Moreover, you may declare unto them, that if they deliver you not, I will not leave a man alive in their country. And thus, if one of you can come to speak with me, they shall have either the man, woman, or child in pawn for you. And thus unto God, whom I trust you do serve, in haste I leave you, and to Him we will daily pray for you. This Tuesday morning, the seventh of August, Anno 1577.

Yours to the uttermost of my power

MARTIN FROBISHER.

I have sent you by these bearers, pen, ink, and paper, to write back unto me again, if personally you cannot come to certify me of your estate.'

Now had the General altered his determination for going any further into the straits at this time,

for any further discovery of the passage, having taken
a man and a woman of that country, which he thought
sufficient for the use of language; and having also
met with these people here, which intercepted his
men the last year, (as the apparel and English furniture,
which was found in their tents, very well declared)
he knew it was but a labour lost to seek them further
off, when he had found them there at hand. And
considering also the short time he had in hand, he
thought it best to bend his whole endeavour for the
getting of mine, and to leave the passage further to be
discovered hereafter. For his commission directed him
in this voyage, only for the searching of the ore, and
to defer the further discovery of the passage until
another time.

On Thursday, the ninth of August, we began to make
a small fort for our defence in the Countess's Island,
and entrenched a corner of a cliff, which on three
parts, like a wall of good height, was compassed and
well fenced with the sea.

Saturday, the eleventh of August, the people shewed
themselves again, and called unto us from the side
of a hill over against us. The General (with good
hope to hear of his men, and to have answer of his
letter) went over unto them, where they presented
themselves not above three in sight, but were hidden
indeed in greater numbers behind the rocks; and making
signs of delay with us, to entrap some of us to redeem
their own, did only seek advantage to train our boat
about a point of land from sight of our company.
Whereupon our men, justly suspecting them, kept
aloof without their danger, and yet set one of our
company ashore, which took up a great bladder which

one of them offered us, and leaving a looking-glass
in the place, came into the boat again. In the mean-
while, our men which stood in the Countess's Island
to behold, who might better discern them, than those
of the boat, by reason they were on higher ground,
made a great outcry unto our men in the boat, for
that they saw divers of the savages creeping behind
the rocks towards our men; whereupon the General
presently returned without tidings of his men.

Concerning this bladder which we received, our
captive made signs that it was given him to keep
water and drink in; but we suspected rather it was
given him to swim and shift away withal, for he and
the woman sought divers times to escape, having
loosed our boats from astern our ships, and we never
a boat left to pursue them withal, and had prevailed
very far, had they not been very timely espied and
prevented therein.

After our General's coming away from them they
mustered themselves in our sight, upon the top of
a hill, to the number of twenty in a rank, all holding
hands over their heads, and dancing with great noise
and songs together. We supposed they made this
dance and shew for us to understand, that we might
take view of their whole companies and force, meaning
belike that we should do the same. And thus they
continued upon the hill tops until night, when hearing
a piece of our great ordnance, which thundered in the
hollowness of the high hills, it made unto them so
fearful a noise, that they had no great will to tarry
long after. And this was done more to make them
know our force than to do them any hurt at all.

On Sunday, the 12 of August, Captain Fenton

trained the company, and made the soldiers maintain skirmish among themselves, as well for their exercise, as for the country people to behold in what readiness our men were always to be found; for it was to be thought, that they lay hid in the hills thereabout, and observed all the manner of our proceedings.

On Wednesday, the fourteenth of August, our General with two small boats well appointed, for that he suspected the country people to lie lurking thereabout, went up a certain bay within the Countess's Sound, to search for ore, and met again with the country people; who so soon as they saw our men made great outcries, and with a white flag made of bladders sewed together with the guts and sinews of beasts, wafted us amain unto them, but shewed not above three of their company. But when we came near them, we might perceive a great multitude creeping behind the rocks, which gave us good cause to suspect their traitorous meaning: whereupon we made them signs, that if they would lay their weapons aside, and come forth, we would deal friendly with them, although their intent was manifested unto us. But for all the signs of friendship we could make them, they came still creeping towards us behind the rocks to get more advantage of us, as though we had no eyes to see them, thinking belike that our single wits could not discover so bare devices and simple drifts of theirs. Their spokesman earnestly persuaded us with many enticing shews, to come eat and sleep ashore, with great arguments of courtesy; and clapping his bare hands over his head in token of peace and innocency, willed us to do the like. But the better to allure our hungry stomachs, he brought us a trim bait of raw

flesh, which for fashion sake with a boat-hook we
caught into our boat : but when the cunning cater
perceived his first cold morsel could nothing sharpen
our stomachs, he cast about for a new train of warm
flesh to procure our appetites. Wherefore he caused
one of his fellows, in halting manner, to come forth
as a lame man from behind the rocks ; and the better
to declare his kindness in carving, he hoised him upon
his shoulders, and bringing him hard to the water
side where we were, left him there limping as an easy
prey to be taken of us. His hope was that we would
bite at this bait, and speedily leap ashore within
their danger ; whereby they might have apprehended
some of us, to ransom their friends home again, which
before we had taken. The gentlemen and soldiers had
great will to encounter them ashore, but the General
more careful by process of time to win them, than
wilfully at the first to spoil them, would in no wise
admit that any man should put himself in hazard
ashore, considering the matter he now intended was
for the ore, and not for the conquest. Notwithstanding,
to prove this cripple's footmanship, he gave liberty
for one to shoot. Whereupon the cripple, having a
parting blow, lightly recovered a rock, and went away
a true and no feigned cripple, and hath learned his
lesson, for ever halting afore such cripples again. But
his fellows which lay hid before, full quickly then
appeared in their likeness, and maintained the skirmish
with their slings, bows and arrows very fiercely,
and came as near as the water suffered them : and
with as desperate mind as hath been seen in any men,
without fear of shot or anything, followed us all along
the coast ; but all their shot fell short of us, and are

of little danger. They had belayed all the coast along for us, and being dispersed so, were not well to be numbered, but we might discern of them above an hundred persons, and had cause to suspect a greater number. And thus without loss or hurt we returned to our ships again.

Now our work growing to an end, and having, only with five poor miners, and the help of a few gentlemen and soldiers, brought aboard almost two hundred ton of ore in the space of twenty days, every man therewithal well comforted, determined lustily to work afresh for a boon voyage, to bring our labour to a speedy and happy end.

And upon Wednesday at night, being the one and twentieth of August, we fully finished the whole work. And it was now good time to leave, for as the men were well wearied, so their shoes and clothes were well worn, their baskets' bottoms torn out, their tools broken, and the ships reasonably well filled. Some with over-straining themselves received hurts not a little dangerous. And about this time the ice began to congeal and freeze about our ships' sides a-night, which gave us a good argument of the sun's declining southward, and put us in mind to make more haste homeward.

Thursday, the 22 of August, we plucked down our tents and every man hasted homeward, and making bonfires upon the top of the highest mount of the island, and marching with ensign displayed round about the island, we gave a volley of shot for a farewell, in honour of the Right Honourable Lady Anne, Countess of Warwick, whose name it beareth : and so departed aboard.

The 23 of August, having the wind large at west, we set sail from out of the Countess's Sound homeward ; but the wind calming we came to anchor within the point of the same sound again.

The 24 of August about three of the clock in the morning, having the wind large at west, we set sail again, and by nine of the clock at night we left the Queen's Foreland astern of us, and being clear of the straits, we bare further into the main ocean, keeping our course more southerly, to bring ourselves the sooner under the latitude of our own climate.   The wind was very great at sea, so that we lay a-hull all night, and had snow half a foot deep on the hatches.

From the 24 until the 28 we had very much wind, but large, keeping our course south-south-east, and had like to have lost the barks, but by good hap we met again.   The height being taken, we were in [cipher] degrees and a half.

The 29 of August the wind blew much at north-east, so that we could bear but only a bunt of our foresail, and the barks were not able to carry any sail at all.   The *Michael* lost company of us, and shaped her course towards Orkney, because that way was better known unto them, and arrived at Yarmouth.

The 30 of August, with the force of the wind, and a surge of the sea, the master of the *Gabriel* and the boatswain were stricken both overboard, and hardly was the boatswain recovered, having hold on a rope hanging overboard in the sea ; and yet the bark was laced fore and after with ropes a breast high within board.   This master was called William Smith, being but a young man and a very sufficient mariner. Who being all the morning before exceeding pleasant, told his captain he dreamed that he was cast overboard, and that the boatswain had him by the hand, and could not save him. And so, immediately upon the end of his tale, his dream came right evilly to pass : and indeed the boatswain in like sort held him by one hand, having hold on a rope with the other, until his force failed, and the master drowned. The height being taken we found ourselves to be in the latitude of [cipher] degrees and a half, and reckoned ourselves from the Queen's Cape homeward about two hundred leagues.

The last of August, about midnight, we had two or three great and sudden flaws or storms.

The first of September the storm was grown very great, and continued almost the whole day and night, and lying a-hull to tarry for the barks our ship was much beaten with the seas, every sea almost overtaking our poop, so that we were constrained with a bunt of our sail to try it out, and ease the rolling of our ship. And so the *Gabriel* not able to bear any sail to keep company with us, and our ship being higher in the poop, and a tall ship, whereon the wind had more force to drive, went so fast away that we lost sight of them, and left them to God and their good fortune of sea. The second day of September in the morning, it pleased God of his goodness to send us a calm, whereby we perceived the rudder of our ship torn in twain, and almost ready to fall away. Wherefore, taking the benefit of the time, we flung half-a-dozen couple of our best men overboard, who taking great pains under water, driving planks, and binding with ropes, did well strengthen and mend the matter who returned the most part more than

half-dead out of the water, and as God's pleasure
was, the sea was calm until the work was finished.

The seventeenth of September we sounded, and had
forty fathom, and were not far off the Land's-End,
finding branded sand with small worms and cockle-
shells, and were shot between Scilly and the Land's-End;
and being within the bay, we were not able to double
the point with a south-and-by-east way, but were
fain to make another board, the wind being at south-
west and by west, and yet could not double the point
to come clear of the Land's-End, to bear along the
Channel: and the weather cleared up when we were
hard aboard the shore, and we made the Land's-End
perfect, and so put up along Saint George's Channel.
And the weather being very foul at sea, we coveted
some harbour, because our steerage was broken,
and so came to anchor in Padstow Road, in Cornwall.
But riding there a very dangerous road, we were
advised by the country to put to sea again, and of the
two evils, to choose the less, for there was nothing
but present peril where we rode. Whereupon we plied
along the Channel to get to Lundy, from whence we
were again driven, being but an open road, where
our anchor came home; and with force of weather
put to seas again, and about the three and twentieth of
September arrived at Milford Haven, in Wales, which
being a very good harbour, made us happy men, that
we had received such long-desired safety.

About one month after our arrival here, by order
from the Lords of the Council, the ship came up to
Bristow, where the ore was committed to keeping
in the castle there. Here we found the *Gabriel*, one
of the barks, arrived in good safety, who having

never a man within board very sufficient to bring
home the ship, after the master was lost, by good
fortune, when she came upon the coast, met with a
ship of Bristow at sea, who conducted her in safety
thither.

Here we heard good tidings also of the arrival of
the other bark called the *Michael*, in the north parts,
which was not a little joyful unto us, that it pleased
God so to bring us to a safe meeting again; and we
lost in all the voyage only one man, besides one that
died at sea, which was sick before he came aboard,
and was so desirous to follow this enterprise that
he rather chose to die therein than not to be one
to attempt so notable a voyage.

DAVIS. FIRST VOYAGE

The first voyage of Master John Davis, undertaken in June 1585, for the discovery of the North-west passage. Written by Master John Jane, merchant, sometime servant to the worshipful Master William Sanderson.

Certain honourable personages and worthy gentlemen of the court and country, with divers worshipful merchants of London and of the west country, moved with desire to advance God's glory and to seek the good of their native country, consulting together of the likelihood of the discovery of the North-west passage, which heretofore had been attempted, but unhappily given over by accidents unlooked for, which turned the enterprisers from their principal purpose, resolved after good deliberation, to put down their adventures to provide for necessary shipping, and a fit man to be chief conductor of this so hard an enterprise. The setting forth of this action was committed by the adventurers especially to the care of Master William Sanderson, merchant of London, who was so forward therein, that besides his travail, which was not small, he became the greatest adventurer with his purse; and commended unto the rest of the company one Master John Davis, a man very well grounded in the principles of the art of navigation for captain and chief pilot of this exploit.

Thus therefore all things being put in a readiness, we departed from Dartmouth the seventh of June, towards the discovery of the aforesaid north-west passage, with two barks, the one being of 50 tons, named the *Sunshine* of London, and the other being 35 tons, named the *Moonshine* of Dartmouth. In the *Sunshine* we had 23 persons, whose names are these following : Master John Davis, captain, William Eston, master, Richard Pope, master's mate, John Jane, merchant, Henry Davy, gunner, William Crosse, boatswain, John Bagge, Walter Arthur, Luke Adams, Robert Coxworthy, John Ellis, John Kelley, Edward Helman, William Dicke, Andrew Maddocke, Thomas Hill, Robert Watts, carpenter, William Russell, Christopher Gorney, boy : James Cole, Francis Ridley, John Russell, Robert Cornish, musicians.

The *Moonshine* had 19 persons: William Bruton, captain, John Ellis, master, the rest, mariners.

The first of July we saw a great store of porpoises. The master called for an harping iron, and shot twice or thrice : sometimes he missed, and at last shot one and struck him in the side, and wound him into the ship. When we had him aboard, the master said it was a darlyhead.

The 2 we had some of the fish sodden, and it did eat as sweet as any mutton.

The 3 we had more in sight, and the master went to shoot at them, but they were so great that they burst our irons, and we lost both fish, irons, pastime, and all. Yet nevertheless the master shot at them with a pike, and had well nigh gotten one, but he was so strong that he burst off the bars of the pike and went away. Then he took the boat-hook and hit one with that, but all would not prevail, so at length we let them alone.

The 6 we saw a very great whale, and every day we saw whales continually.

The 16, 17, and 18, we saw great store of whales.

The 19 of July we fell into a great whirling and brustling of a tide, setting to the northwards; and sailing about half a league, we came into a very calm sea, which bent to the south-south-west. Here we heard a mighty great roaring of the sea, as if it had been the breach of some shore, the air being so foggy and full of thick mist, that we could not see the one ship from the other, being a very small distance asunder. So the captain and the master, being in distrust how the tide might set them, caused the *Moonshine* to hoise out her boat and to sound; but they could not find ground in 300 fathoms and better. Then the captain, master, and I went towards the breach to see what it should be, giving charge to our gunners that at every glass they should shoot off a musket-shot, to the intent we might keep ourselves from losing them. Then, coming near to the breach, we met many islands of ice floating, which had quickly compassed us about. Then we went upon some of them, and did perceive that all the roaring which we heard, was caused only by the rolling of this ice together. Our company, seeing us not to return according to our appointment, left off shooting muskets and began to shoot falconets; for they feared some mishap had befallen us. But before night we came aboard again with our boat laden with ice, which made very good fresh water. Then we bent our course toward the north, hoping by that means to double the land.

The 20, as we sailed along the coast, the fog broke up, and we discovered the land, which was the most deformed, rocky, and mountainous land that ever we saw. The first sight whereof did shew as if it had been in form of a sugar-loaf, standing to our sight above the clouds; for that it did shew over the fog like a white list in the sky, the tops altogether covered with snow, and the shore beset with ice a league off into the sea, making such irksome noise, as that it seemed to be the true pattern of desolation; and after the same our captain named it, The Land of Desolation.

Upon Thursday, being the 22 of this month, about three of the clock in the morning, we hoised out our boat, and the captain with six sailors went towards the shore, thinking to find a landing place; for the night before we did perceive the coast to be void of ice to our judgment, and the same night we were all persuaded that we had seen a canoa rowing along the shore; but afterwards we fell in some doubt of it, but we had no great reason so to do. The captain rowing towards the shore, willed the master to bear in with the land after him, and before he came near the shore by the space of a league, or about two miles, he found so much ice that he could not get to land by any means. Here our mariners put to their lines to see if they could get any fish, because there were so many seals upon the coast, and the birds did beat upon the water; but all was in vain. The water about this place was very black and thick, like to a filthy standing pool. We sounded and had ground in 120 fathoms. While the captain was rowing to the shore, our men saw woods upon the rocks, like to the rocks of Newfoundland; but I could not discern them. Yet it might be so very well: for we had wood floating upon the coast every day, and the *Moonshine* took up a tree at sea, not far from the coast, being sixty foot of length and fourteen handfuls about, having the root upon it. After this the captain came aboard, the weather being very calm and fair we bent our course toward the south, with intent to double the land.

The 23 we coasted the land, which did lie east-north-east and west-south-west.

The 24, the wind being very fair at east, we coasted the land, which did lie east and west, not being able to come near the shore by reason of the great quantity of ice. At this place, because the weather was somewhat cold by reason of the ice, and the better to encourage our men, their allowance was increased. The captain and the master took order that every mess, being five persons, should have half a pound of bread and a can of beer every morning to breakfast. The weather was not very cold, but the air was moderate like to our April weather in England. When the wind came from the land, or the ice, it was somewhat cold; but when it came off the sea, it was very hot.

The 25 of this month we departed from sight of this land at six of the clock in the morning, directing our course to the north-westward, hoping in God's mercy to find our desired passage; and so continued above four days.

The 29 of July we discovered land in 64 degrees

15 minutes of latitude, bearing north-east from us. The wind being contrary to go to the north-westwards, we bare in with this land to take some view of it, being utterly void of the pester of ice and very temperate. Coming near the coast, we found many fair sounds and good roads for shipping, and many great inlets into the land, whereby we judged this land to be a great number of islands standing together. Here having moored our bark in good order, we went on shore upon a small island to seek for water and wood. Upon this island we did perceive that there had been people : for we found a small shoe and pieces of leather sewed with sinews, and a piece of fur, and wool like to beaver. Then we went upon another island on the other side of our ships ; and the captain, the master, and I, being got up to the top of an high rock, the people of the country having espied us, made a lamentable noise, as we thought, with great outcries and screechings. We, hearing them, thought it had been the howling of wolves. At last I halloaed again, and they likewise cried. Then, we perceiving where they stood, some on the shore, and one rowing in a canoa about a small island fast by them, we made a great noise, partly to allure them to us, and partly to warn our company of them. Whereupon Master Bruton and the master of his ship, with others of their company, made great haste towards us, and brought our musicians with them from our ship, purposing either by force to rescue us, if need should so require, or with courtesy to allure the people. When they came unto us, we caused our musicians to play, ourselves dancing, and making many signs of friendship. At length there came ten canoas from the other islands, and two of them

came so near the shore where we were, that they
talked with us, the others being in their boats a
pretty way off. Their pronunciation was very hollow
through the throat, and their speech such as we could
not understand : only we allured them by friendly
embracings and signs of courtesy. At length one of
them, pointing up to the sun with his hand, would
presently strike his breast so hard that we might
hear the blow. This he did many times before he
would any way trust us. Then John Ellis, the master
of the *Moonshine*, was appointed to use his best policy
to gain their friendship ; who struck his breast, and
pointed to the sun after their order. Which when
he had divers times done, they began to trust him,
and one of them came on shore, to whom we threw
our caps, stockings, and gloves, and such other things
as then we had about us, playing with our music,
and making signs of joy, and dancing. So the night
coming, we bade them farewell, and went aboard our
barks.

The next morning, being the 30 of July, there came
thirty-seven canoas rowing by our ships, calling to us
to come on shore. We not making any great haste
unto them, one of them went up to the top of the
rock, and leapt and danced as they had done the day
before, shewing us a seal's skin, and another thing
made like a timbrel, which he did beat upon with
a stick, making a noise like a small drum. Whereupon
we manned our boats and came to them, they all
staying in their canoas : we came to the water side
where they were, and after we had sworn by the sun
after their fashion, they did trust us. So I shook
hands with one of them, and he kissed my hand,

and we were very familiar with them. We were in so great credit with them upon this single acquaintance, that we could have anything they had. We bought five canoas of them : we bought their clothes from their backs, which were all made of seals' skins and birds' skins ; their buskins, their hose, their gloves, all being commonly sewed and well dressed : so that we were fully persuaded that they have divers artificers among them. We had a pair of buskins of them full of fine wool like beaver. Their apparel for heat was made of birds' skins with their feathers on them. We saw among them leather dressed like glover's leather, and thick thongs like white leather of a good length. We had of their darts and oars, and found in them that they would by no means displease us, but would give us whatsoever we asked of them, and would be satisfied with whatsoever we gave them. They took great care one of another : for when we had bought their boats, then two other would come and carry him away between them that had sold us his. They are very tractable people, void of craft or double dealing, and easy to be brought to any civility or good order : but we judge them to be idolaters and to worship the sun.

During the time of our abode among these islands we found reasonable quantity of wood, both fir, spruce, and juniper ; which, whether it came floating any great distance to these places where we found it, or whether it grew in some great islands near the same place by us not yet discovered, we know not ; but we judge that it groweth there further into the land than we were, because the people had great store of darts and oars which they made none account of, but gave them to us for small trifles, as points and pieces of paper. We saw about this coast marvellous great abundance of seals sculling together like sculls of small fish. We found no fresh water among these islands, but only snow-water, whereof we found great pools. The cliffs were all of such ore as Master Frobisher brought from Meta Incognita. We had divers shows of study, or Muscovy glass, shining not altogether unlike to crystal. We found an herb growing upon the rocks, whose fruit was sweet, full of red juice, and the ripe ones were like corinths. We found also birch and willow growing like shrubs low to the ground. These people have great store of furs, as we judge. They made shows unto us the 30 of this present (which was the second time of our being with them), after they perceived we would have skins and furs, that they would go into the country and come again the next day with such things as they had. But this night the wind coming fair, the captain and the master would by no means detract the purpose of our discovery. And so the last of this month about four of the clock in the morning in God's Name we set sail, and were all that day becalmed upon the coast.

The first of August we had a fair wind, and so proceeded towards the north-west for our discovery.

The sixth of August we discovered land in 66 degrees 40 minutes of latitude, altogether void from the pester of ice : we anchored in a very fair road under a brave mount, the cliffs whereof were as orient as gold. This mount was named Mount Raleigh. The road where our ships lay at anchor was called Totnes Road. The sound which did compass the mount was named Exeter Sound. The foreland towards the

north was called Dyer's Cape. The foreland towards
the south was named Cape Walsingham. So soon
as we were come to an anchor in Totnes Road under
Mount Raleigh, we espied four white bears at the
foot of the mount. We supposing them to be goats
or wolves, manned our boats and went towards them;
but when we came near the shore, we found them to
be white bears of a monstrous bigness. We being
desirous of fresh victuals and the sport, began to
assault them, and I being on land, one of them came
down the hill right against me. My piece was charged
with hailshot and a bullet: I discharged my piece
and shot him in the neck; he roared a little, and took
the water straight, making small account of his hurt.
Then we followed him with our boat, and killed him
with boar-spears, and two more that night.

The 7 we went on shore to another bear which
lay all night upon the top of an island under Mount
Raleigh, and when we came up to him he lay fast
asleep. I levelled at his head, and the stone of my
piece gave no fire: with that he looked up, and laid
down his head again. Then I shot, being charged
with two bullets, and struck him in the head: he
being but amazed fell backwards. Whereupon we
ran all upon him with boar-spears, and thrust him
in the body: yet for all that he gript away our boar-
spears, and went towards the water; and as he was
going down, he came back again. Then our master
shot his boar-spear, and struck him in the head,
and made him to take the water, and swim into a
cove fast by, where we killed him, and brought him
aboard. The breadth of his forefoot from one side
to the other was fourteen inches over. They were

very fat, so as we were constrained to cast the fat
away. We saw a raven upon Mount Raleigh. We
found withies also growing like low shrubs, and flowers
like primroses in the said place. The coast is very
mountainous, altogether without wood, grass, or earth,
and is only huge mountains of stone ; but the bravest
stone that ever we saw. The air was very moderate
in this country.

The 8 we departed from Mount Raleigh, coasting
along the shore, which lieth south-south-west, and
east-north-east.

The 9 our men fell in dislike of their allowance,
because it was too small as they thought. Whereupon
we made a new proportion : every mess, being five
to a mess, should have four pound of bread a day,
twelve wine quarts of beer, six Newland fishes ; and
the flesh days a gill of pease more. So we restrained
them from their butter and cheese.

The 11 we came to the most southerly cape
of this land, which we named The Cape of God's
Mercy, as being the place of our first entrance for
the discovery. The weather being very foggy we
coasted this north land. At length when it brake
up, we perceived that we were shot into a very fair
entrance or passage, being in some places twenty
leagues broad, and in some thirty, altogether void
of any pester of ice, the weather very tolerable, and
the water of the very colour, nature, and quality of
the main ocean, which gave us the greater hope of
our passage. Having sailed north-west sixty leagues
in this entrance, we discovered certain islands standing
in the midst thereof, having open passage on both
sides. Whereupon our ships divided themselves, the

one sailing on the north side, the other on the south side of the said isles, where we stayed five days, having the wind at south-east, very foggy and foul weather.

The 14 we went on shore and found signs of people, for we found stones laid up together like a wall, and saw the skull of a man or a woman.

The 15 we heard dogs howl on the shore, which we thought had been wolves, and therefore we went on shore to kill them. When we came on land the dogs came presently to our boat very gently, yet we thought they came to prey upon us, and therefore we shot at them, and killed two: and about the neck of one of them we found a leather collar, whereupon we thought them to be tame dogs. Then we went farther, and found two sleds made like ours in England: the one was made of fir, spruce, and oaken boards sawn like inch boards: the other was made all of whale-bone, and there hung on the tops of the sleds three heads of beasts which they had killed. We saw here larks, ravens, and partridges.

The 17 we went on shore, and in a little thing made like an oven with stones I found many small trifles, as a small canoa made of wood, a piece of wood made like an image, a bird made of bone, beads having small holes in one end of them to hang about their necks, and other small things. The coast was very barren without wood or grass: the rocks were very fair like marble, full of veins of divers colours. We found a seal which was killed not long before, being flean, and hid under stones.

Our captain and master searched still for probabilities of the passage ; and first, found that this place was all islands, with great sounds passing between them.

Secondly, the water remained of one colour with the main ocean without altering.

Thirdly, we saw to the west of those isles three or four whales in a scull, which they judged to come from a westerly sea, because to the eastward we saw not any whale.

Also, as we were rowing into a very great sound lying south-west, from whence these whales came, upon the sudden there came a violent counter-check of a tide from the south-west against the flood which we came with, not knowing from whence it was maintained.

Fifthly, in sailing twenty leagues within the mouth of this entrance we had sounding in 90 fathoms, fair grey oozy sand, and the further we ran into the westwards the deeper was the water ; so that hard aboard the shore among these isles we could not have ground in 330 fathoms.

Lastly, it did ebb and flow six or seven fathom up and down, the flood coming from divers parts, so as we could not perceive the chief maintenance thereof.

The 18 and 19 our captain and master determined what was best to do, both for the safeguard of their credits, and satisfying of the adventurers, and resolved, if the weather brake up, to make further search.

The 20 the wind came directly against us : so they altered their purpose, and reasoned both for proceeding and returning.

The 21, the wind being north-west, we departed from these islands ; and as we coasted the south shore we saw many fair sounds, whereby we were persuaded that it was no firm land but islands.

The 23 of this month the wind came south-east, with very stormy and foul weather : so we were constrained to seek harbour upon the south coast of this entrance, where we fell into a very fair sound, and anchored in 25 fathoms green oozy sand.   Here we went on shore, where we had manifest signs of people, where they had made their fire, and laid stones like a wall.   In this place we saw four very fair falcons ; and Master Bruton took from one of them his prey, which we judged by the wings and legs to be a snite, for the head was eaten off.

The 24 in the afternoon, the wind coming somewhat fair, we departed from this road, purposing by God's grace to return for England.

The 26 we departed from sight of the north land of this entrance, directing our course homewards until the tenth of the next month.

The 10 of September we fell with The Land of Desolation, thinking to go on shore, but we could get never a good harbour.   That night we put to sea again, thinking to search it the next day ; but this night arose a very great storm, and separated our ships, so that we lost the sight of the *Moonshine*.

The 13 about noon (having tried all the night before with a goose wing) we set sail, and within two hours after, we had sight of the *Moonshine* again.   This day we departed from this land.

The 27 of this month we fell with sight of England. This night we had a marvellous storm and lost the *Moonshine*.

The 30 of September we came into Dartmouth, where we found the *Moonshine*, being come in not two hours before.

DAVIS.   SECOND VOYAGE

(By Himself)

The second voyage attempted by Master John Davis
with others, for the discovery of the North-west
passage, in Anno 1586.

The 7 day of May I departed from the port of
Dartmouth for the discovery of the North-west passage, with a ship of an hundred-and-twenty tons named
the *Mermaid*, a bark of 60 tons named the *Sunshine*,
a bark of 35 tons named the *Moonshine*, and a pinnace
of 10 tons named the *North Star*.

And the 15 of June I discovered land in the latitude of 60 degrees, and in longitude from the meridian
of London westward 47 degrees, mightily pestered
with ice and snow, so that there was no hope of
landing. The ice lay in some places ten leagues, in
some twenty, and in some fifty leagues off the shore,
so that we were constrained to bear into 57 degrees
to double the same, and to recover a free sea, which
through God's favourable mercy we at length obtained.

The 29 of June after many tempestuous storms we
again discovered land, in longitude from the meridian
of London 58 degrees 30 minutes, and in latitude 64,
being east from us. Into which course, sith it please
God by contrary winds to force us, I thought it very

necessary to bear in with it, and there to set up our pinnace, provided in the *Mermaid* to be our scout for this discovery; and so much the rather, because the year before I had been in the same place, and found it very convenient for such a purpose, well stored with float-wood, and possessed by a people of tractable conversation : so that the 29 of this month we arrived within the isles which lay before this land, lying north-north-west, and south-south-east, we know not how far. This land is very high and mountainous, having before it on the west side a mighty company of isles full of fair sounds, and harbours. This land was very little troubled with snow, and the sea altogether void of ice.

The ships being within the sounds, we sent our boats to search for shoal-water, where we might anchor, which in this place is very hard to find ; and as the boat went sounding and searching, the people of the country having espied them, came in their canoas towards them with many shouts and cries. But after they had espied in the boat some of our company that were the year before here with us, they presently rowed to the boat, and took hold on the oar, and hung about the boat with such comfortable joy, as would require a long discourse to be uttered. They came with the boats to our ships, making signs that they knew all those that the year before had been with them. After I perceived their joy and small fear of us, myself with the merchants and others of the company went ashore, bearing with me twenty knives. I had no sooner landed, but they leapt out of their canoas and came running to me and the rest, and embraced us with many signs of hearty welcome.

At this present there were eighteen of them, and
to each of them I gave a knife.   They offered skins
to me for reward, but I made signs that they were
not sold, but given them of courtesy ; and so dismissed
them for that time, with signs that they should return
again after certain hours.

The next day with all possible speed the pinnace
was landed upon an isle, there to be finished to serve
our purpose for the discovery.   Which isle was so convenient for that purpose, as that we were very well
able to defend ourselves against many enemies.   During
the time that the pinnace was there setting up, the
people came continually unto us, sometime an hundred
canoas at a time, sometime forty, fifty, more and less,
as occasion served.   They brought with them seal
skins, stag skins, white hares, seal fish, salmon peel,
small cod, dry capelin, with other fish, and birds such
as the country did yield.

Myself still desirous to have a further search
of this place, sent one of the ship-boats to one part of
the land, and myself went to another part to search
for the habitation of this people, with straight commandment that there should be no injury offered to any
of the people, neither any gun shot.

The boats that went from me found the tents
of the people made with seal skins set up upon timber,
wherein they found great store of dried capelin, being
a little fish no bigger than a pilchard : they found
bags of train oil, many little images cut in wood,
seal skins in tan-tubs, with many other such trifles,
whereof they diminished nothing.

They also found ten miles within the snowy mountains a plain champaign country, with earth and grass,

such as our moory and waste grounds of England are. They went up into a river (which in the narrowest place is two leagues broad) about ten leagues, finding it still to continue they knew not how far. But I with my company took another river, which although at the first it offered a large inlet, yet it proved but a deep bay, the end whereof in four hours I attained ; and there leaving the boat well manned, went with the rest of my company three or four miles into the country, but found nothing, nor saw anything, save only gripes, ravens, and small birds, as larks and linnets.

The third of July I manned my boat, and went with fifty canoas attending upon me up into another sound, where the people by signs willed me to go, hoping to find their habitation. At length they made signs that I should go into a warm place to sleep. At which place I went on shore, and ascended the top of a high hill to see into the country, but perceiving my labour vain, I returned again to my boat, the people still following me and my company, very diligent to attend us, and to help us up the rocks, and likewise down. At length I was desirous to have our men leap with them, which was done, but our men did overleap them : from leaping they went to wrestling. We found them strong and nimble, and to have skill in wrestling, for they cast some of our men that were good wrestlers.

The fourth of July we launched our pinnace, and had forty of the people to help us, which they did very willingly. At this time our men again wrestled with them, and found them as before, strong and skilful. This fourth of July the master of the *Mermaid* went to certain islands to store himself with wood, where he found a grave with divers buried in it, only covered with seal skins, having a cross laid over them. The people are of good stature, well in body proportioned, with small slender hands and feet, with broad visages, and small eyes, wide mouths, the most part unbearded, great lips, and close toothed. Their custom is, as often as they go from us, still at their return to make a new truce, in this sort. Holding his hand up to the sun, with a loud voice he crieth "Iliaout," and striketh his breast: with like signs being promised safety, he giveth credit. These people are much given to bleed, and therefore stop their noses with deer's hair, or the hair of an elan. They are idolaters and have images great store, which they wear about them, and in their boats, which we suppose they worship. They are witches, and have many kinds of enchantments, which they often used; but to small purpose, thanks be to God.

Being among them at shore the fourth of July, one of them, making a long oration, began to kindle a fire in this manner. He took a piece of a board wherein was a hole half through: into that hole he puts the end of a round stick like unto a bedstaff, wetting the end thereof in train, and in fashion of a turner with a piece of leather, by his violent motion doth very speedily produce fire. Which done, with turfs he made a fire, into which with many words and strange gestures he put divers things, which we supposed to be a sacrifice. Myself and divers of my company standing by, they were desirous to have me go into the smoke. I willed them likewise to stand in the smoke, which they by no means would

do. I then took one of them, and thrust him into
the smoke, and willed one of my company to tread out
the fire, and to spurn it into the sea, which was done
to show them that we did contemn their sorcery.
These people are very simple in all their conversation,
but marvellous thievish, especially for iron, which
they have in great account. They began through
our lenity to show their vile nature. They began to
cut our cables: they cut away the *Moonshine's* boat
from her stern: they cut our cloth where it lay to
air, though we did carefully look unto it: they stole
our oars, a caliver, a boar-spear, a sword, with divers
other things. Whereat the company and masters being
grieved, for our better security desired me to dis-
solve this new friendship, and to leave the company
of these thievish miscreants. Whereupon there was
a caliver shot among them, and immediately upon
the same a falcon, which strange noise did sore
amaze them, so that with speed they departed. Notwithstanding, their simplicity is such, that within
ten hours after they came again to us to entreat peace ;
which being promised, we again fell into a great league.
They brought us seal skins, and salmon peel; but
seeing iron, they could in no wise forbear stealing.
Which when I perceived, it did but minister unto me
an occasion of laughter, to see their simplicity, and
I willed that in no case they should be any more hardly
used, but that our own company should be the more
vigilant to keep their things, supposing it to be very
hard in so short time to make them know their evils.
They eat all their meat raw: they live most upon
fish : they drink salt water, and eat grass and ice
with delight. They are never out of the water, but

live in the nature of fishes, save only when dead sleep taketh them, and then under a warm rock laying his boat upon the land, he lieth down to sleep. Their weapons are all darts, but some of them have bow and arrows and slings. They make nets to take their fish, of the fin of a whale. They do all their things very artificially : and it should seem that these simple thievish islanders have war with those of the main, for many of them are sore wounded, which wounds they received upon the mainland, as by signs they gave us to understand. We had among them copper ore, black copper, and red copper. They pronounce their language very hollow, and deep in the throat.

The seventh of July, being very desirous to search the habitation of this country, I went myself with our new pinnace into the body of the land, thinking it to be a firm continent ; and passing up a very large river, a great flaw of wind took me, whereby we were constrained to seek succour for that night. Which being had, I landed with the most part of my company, and went to the top of a high mountain, hoping from thence to see into the country : but the mountains were so many and so mighty as that my purpose prevailed not. Whereupon I again returned to my pinnace, and willing divers of my company to gather mussels for my supper, whereof in this place there was great store, myself having espied a very strange sight, especially to me that never before saw the like, which was a mighty whirlwind taking up the water in very great quantity, furiously mounting it into the air. Which whirlwind was not for a puff or blast, but continual, for the space of three hours, with very little intermission. Which sith it was in the course that I should pass, we were constrained that night to take up our lodging under the rocks.

The next morning the storm being broken up, we went forward in our attempt, and sailed into a mighty great river directly into the body of the land; and in brief, found it to be no firm land, but huge, waste, and desert isles with mighty sounds, and inlets passing between sea and sea. Whereupon we returned towards our ships, and landing to stop a flood, we found the burial of these miscreants. We found of their fish in bags, plaice and capelin dried, of which we took only one bag and departed. The ninth of this month we came to our ships, where we found the people desirous, in their fashion, of friendship and barter. Our mariners complained heavily against the people, and said that my lenity and friendly using of them gave them stomach to mischief : "For they have stolen an anchor from us : they have cut our cable very dangerously : they have cut our boats from our stern ; and now, since your departure, with slings they spare us not with stones of half a pound weight : and will you still endure these injuries ? It is a shame to bear them." I desired them to be content, and said, I doubted not but that all should be well. The 10 of this month I went to the shore, the people following me in their canoas. I tolled them on shore, and used them with much courtesy, and then departed aboard, they following me and my company. I gave some of them bracelets, and caused seven or eight of them to come aboard, which they did willingly, and some of them went into the top of the ship ; and thus courteously using them, I let them depart. The sun was no sooner down, but they began to practise their devilish nature, and with slings threw stones very fiercely into the *Moonshine*, and struck one of her men then boatswain, that he overthrew withal. Whereat being moved, I changed my courtesy, and grew to hatred. Myself in my own boat well manned with shot, and the bark's boat likewise, pursued them, and gave them divers shot, but to small purpose, by reason of their swift rowing : so smally content we returned.

The 11 of this month there came five of them to make a new truce. The master of the Admiral came to me to show me of their coming, and desired to have them taken and kept as prisoners until we had his anchor again. But when he saw that the chief ringleader and master of mischief was one of the five, he then was vehement to execute his purpose, so it was determined to take him. He came crying " Iliaout," and striking his breast offered a pair of gloves to sell : the master offered him a knife for them. So two of them came to us : the one was not touched, but the other was soon captive among us. Then we pointed to him and his fellows for our anchor, which being had, we made signs that he should be set at liberty. Within one hour after he came aboard the wind came fair, whereupon we weighed and set sail, and so brought the fellow with us : one of his fellows still following our ship close aboard, talked with him and made a kind of lamentation, we still using him well with " Iliaout," which was the common course of courtesy. At length this fellow aboard us spake four or five words unto the other and clapped his two hands upon his face, whereupon the other doing the like, departed as we suppose with heavy cheer. We judged the covering of his face with his hands and bowing of his body down, signified his death. At length he became a pleasant companion among us. I gave him a new suit of frieze after the English fashion, because I saw he could not endure the cold, of which he was very joyful. He trimmed up his darts, and all his fishing tools, and would make oakum, and set his hand to a rope's end upon occasion. He lived with the dry capelin that I took when I was searching in the pinnace, and did eat dry Newland fish.

All this while, God be thanked, our people were in very good health, only one young man excepted, who died at sea the fourteenth of this month, and the fifteenth, according to the order of the sea, with praise given to God by service, was cast overboard.

The 17 of this month being in the latitude of 63 degrees 8 minutes, we fell upon a most mighty and strange quantity of ice in one entire mass, so big as that we knew not the limits thereof, and being withal so very high in form of a land, with bays and capes and like high cliff-land, as that we supposed it to be land, and therefore sent our pinnace off to discover it : but at her return we were certainly informed that it was only ice, which bred great admiration to us all considering the huge quantity thereof, incredible to be reported in truth as it was, and therefore I omit to speak any further thereof. This only I think, that the like before was never seen : and in this place we had very stickle and strong currents.

We coasted this mighty mass of ice until the 30 of July, finding it a mighty bar to our purpose. The air in this time was so contagious and the sea

so pestered with ice, as that all hope was banished
of proceeding ; for the 24 of July all our shrouds,
ropes, and sails were so frozen, and compassed with
ice, only by a gross fog, as seemed to me more than
strange, sith the last year I found this sea free and
navigable, without impediments.

Our men through this extremity began to grow
sick and feeble, and withal hopeless of good success :
whereupon very orderly, with good discretion they
entreated me to regard the state of this business,
and withal advised me, that in conscience I ought
to regard the safety of mine own life with the preserva-
tion of theirs, and that I should not through my over-
boldness leave their widows and fatherless children
to give me bitter curses. This matter in conscience
did greatly move me to regard their estates : yet
considering the excellency of the business, if it might
be attained, the great hope of certainty by the last
year's discovery, and that there was yet a third way
not put in practice, I thought it would grow to my
great disgrace, if this action by my negligence should
grow into discredit. Whereupon, seeking help from
God, the fountain of all mercies, it pleased His divine
Majesty to move my heart to prosecute that which
I hope shall be to His glory, and to the contentation
of every Christian mind. Whereupon, falling into
consideration that the *Mermaid*, albeit a very strong
and sufficient ship, yet by reason of her burthen
was not so convenient and nimble as a smaller bark,
especially in such desperate hazards : further, having
in account her great charge to the adventurers, being
at £100 the month, and that in doubtful service :
all the premises considered with divers other things,

I determined to furnish the *Moonshine* with revictualling
and sufficient men, and to proceed in this action as
God should direct me. Whereupon I altered our
course from the ice, and bare east-south-east to recover
the next shore where this thing might be performed.
So with favourable wind it pleased God that the first
of August we discovered the land in latitude 66 degrees
33 minutes, and in longitude from the meridian of
London 70 degrees, void of trouble, without snow
or ice.

The second of August we harboured ourselves
in a very excellent good road, where with all speed
we graved the *Moonshine*, and revictualled her. We
searched this country with our pinnace while the bark
was trimming, which William Eston did. He found
all this land to be only islands, with a sea on the east,
a sea on the west, and a sea on the north. In this
place we found it very hot, and we .were very much
troubled with a fly which is called mosquito, for they
did sting grievously. The people of this place at
our first coming in caught a seal, and with bladders
fast tied to him sent him unto us with the flood, so
as he came right with our ships, which we took as
a friendly present from them.

The fifth of August I went with the two masters
and others to the top of a hill, and by the way William
Eston espied three canoas lying under a rock, and
went unto them. There were in them skins, darts,
with divers superstitious toys, whereof we diminished
nothing, but left upon every boat a silk point, a bullet
of lead, and a pin. The next day, being the sixth
of August, the people came unto us without fear,
and did barter with us for skins, as. the other people

did. They differ not from the other, neither in their
canoas nor apparel, yet is their pronunciation more
plain than the others, and nothing hollow in the throat.
Our savage aboard us kept himself close, and made
show that he would fain have another companion.
Thus being provided, I departed from this land the
twelfth of August at six of the clock in the morning,
where I left the *Mermaid* at an anchor.   The fourteenth,
sailing west about fifty leagues, we discovered land,
being in latitude 66 degrees 19 minutes : this land
is 70 leagues from the other from whence we came.
This fourteenth day from nine o'clock at night till
three o'clock in the morning, we anchored by an
island of ice, twelve leagues off the shore, being moored
to the ice.

The fifteenth day at three o'clock in the morning
we departed from this land to the south, and the
eighteenth of August we discovered land north-west
from us in the morning, being a very fair promontory,
in latitude 65 degrees, having no land on the south.
Here we had great hope of a through passage.

This day at three o'clock in the afternoon we again
discovered land south-west and by south from us,
where at night we were becalmed.   The nineteenth
of this month at noon, by observation, we were in
64 degrees 20 minutes.   From the eighteenth day at
noon unto the nineteenth at noon, by precise ordinary
care, we had sailed 15 leagues south and by west,
yet by art and more exact observation, we found our
course to be south-west, so that we plainly perceived
a great current striking to the west.

This land is nothing in sight but isles, which in-
creaseth our hope.   This nineteenth of August at

six o'clock in the afternoon, it began to snow, and
so continued all night with foul weather, and much
wind, so that we were constrained to lie at hull all
night five leagues off the shore. In the morning being
the twentieth of August, the fog and storm breaking
up, we bare in with the land, and at nine o'clock
in the morning we anchored in a very fair and safe
road and locked for all weathers. At ten of the clock
I went on shore to the top of a very high hill, where I
perceived that this land was islands : at four of the
clock in the afternoon we weighed anchor, having a
fair north-north-east wind, with very fair weather : at
six of the clock we were clear without the land, and so
shaped our course to the south, to discover the coast,
whereby the passage may be through God's mercy found.

We coasted this land till the eight and twentieth
of August, finding it still to continue towards the south,
from the latitude of 67 to 57 degrees. We found
marvellous great store of birds, gulls and mews,
incredible to be reported. Whereupon being calm
weather, we lay one glass upon the lee, to prove for
fish, in which space we caught 100 of cod, although
we were but badly provided for fishing, not being
our purpose. This eight and twentieth having great
distrust of the weather, we arrived in a very fair harbour
in the latitude of 56 degrees, and sailed 10 leagues
into the same, being two leagues broad, with very
fair woods on both sides : in this place we continued
until the first of September, in which time we had
two very great storms. I landed, and went six miles
by guess into the country, and found that the woods
were fir, pine, apple, alder, yew, withy, and birch :
here we saw a black bear. This place yieldeth great

store of birds, as pheasant, partridge, Barbary hens or
the like, wild geese, ducks, blackbirds, jays, thrushes,
with other kinds of small birds.   Of the partridge and
pheasant we killed great store with bow and arrows :
in this place at the harbour mouth we found great
store of cod.

The first of September at ten o'clock we set sail,
and coasted the shore with very fair weather.   The
third day being calm, at noon we struck sail, and let
fall a kedge anchor, to prove whether we could take
any fish, being in latitude 54 degrees 30 minutes ;
in which place we found great abundance of cod, so
that the hook was no sooner overboard, but presently
a fish was taken.   It was the largest and the best
fed fish that ever I saw, and divers fishermen that were
with me said that they never saw a more suavle or
better scull of fish in their lives : yet had they seen
great abundance.

The fourth of September at five o'clock in the
afternoon we anchored in a very good road among great
store of isles, the country lowland, pleasant and very
full of fair woods.   To the north of this place eight
leagues, we had a perfect hope of the passage, finding
a mighty great sea passing between two lands west,
the south land to our judgment being nothing but isles.
We greatly desired to go into this sea, but the wind was
directly against us.   We anchored in four fathom fine
sand.   In this place is fowl and fish mighty store.

The sixth of September having a fair north-north-
west wind, having trimmed our bark we purposed to
depart, and sent five of our sailer's young men ashore
to an island, to fetch certain fish which we purposed
to weather, and therefore left it all night covered

upon the isle. The brutish people of this country lay secretly lurking in the wood, and upon the sudden assaulted our men : which when we perceived, we presently let slip our cables upon the hawse, and under our foresail bare into the shore, and with all expedition discharged a double musket upon them twice, at the noise whereof they fled. Notwithstanding, to our very great grief, two of our men were slain with their arrows, and two grievously wounded, of whom at this present we stand in very great doubt. Only one escaped by swimming, with an arrow shot through his arm. These wicked miscreants never offered parley or speech, but presently executed their cursed fury.

This present evening it pleased God further to increase our sorrows with a mighty tempestuous storm, the wind being north-north-east, which lasted unto the tenth of this month very extreme. We unrigged our ship, and purposed to cut down our masts. The cable of our sheet-anchor brake so that we only expected to be driven on shore among these cannibals for their prey. Yet in this deep distress the mighty mercy of God, when hope was past, gave us succour, and sent us a fair lee, so as we recovered our anchor again, and new moored our ship : where we saw that God manifestly delivered us ; for the strands of one of our cables were broken, and we only rode by an old junk. Thus being freshly moored a new storm arose, the wind being west-north-west, very forcible, which lasted unto the tenth day at night.

The eleventh day with a fair west-north-west wind we departed with trust in God's mercy, shaping our course for England, and arrived in the West country in the beginning of October.

DAVIS. THIRD VOYAGE

The third voyage north-westward, made by Master
John Davis, gentleman, as chief captain and pilot
general, for the discovery of a passage to the isles
of the Moluccas, or the coast of China, in the
year 1587. Written by Master John Jane.

May

The 19 of this present month about midnight we
weighed our anchors, set sail, and departed from
Dartmouth with two barks and a clincher, the one
named the *Elizabeth* of Dartmouth, the other the
Sunshine of London, and the clincher called the *Helen*
of London: thus in God's name we set forwards
with the wind at north-east a good fresh gale. About
three hours after our departure, the night being somewhat thick with darkness, we had lost the pinnace:
the captain imagining that the men had run away
with her, willed the master of the *Sunshine* to stand
to seawards, and see if we could descry them, we
bearing in with the shore for Plymouth. At length
we descried her, bare with her, and demanded what
the cause was: they answered that the tiller of their
helm was burst. So shaping our course west-south-
west, we went forward, hoping that a hard beginning
would make a good ending, yet some of us were doubtful
of it, falling in reckoning that she was a clincher;
nevertheless we put our trust in God.

The 21 we met with the *Red Lion* of London, which came from the coast of Spain, which was afraid that we had been men-of-war; but we hailed them, and after a little conference, we desired the master to carry our letters for London directed to my uncle Sanderson, who promised us a safe delivery. And after we had heaved them a lead and a line, whereunto we had made fast our letters, before they could get them into the ship, they fell into the sea, and so all our labour and theirs also was lost; notwithstanding they promised to certify our departure at London, and so we departed, and the same day we had sight of Scilly.

June

The first six days we had fair weather : after that for five days we had fog and rain, the wind being south. The 12 we had clear weather. The mariners in the *Sunshine* and the master could not agree : the mariners would go on their voyage a-fishing, because the year began to waste : the master would not depart till he had the company of the *Elizabeth*. Whereupon the master told our captain that he was afraid his men would shape some contrary course while he was asleep, and so he should lose us. At length after much talk and many threatenings, they were content to bring us to the land which we looked for daily.

The 14 day we discovered land at five of the clock in the morning, being very great and high mountains, the tops of the hills being covered with snow.

The 16 we came to an anchor about four or five of the clock after noon. The people came presently to us after the old manner, with crying " Iliaout " and showing us seals' skins. The 17 we began to set up the pinnace that Pearson framed at Dartmouth, with the boards which he brought from London.

The 18 Pearson and the carpenters of the ships began to set on the planks. The 19 as we went about an island, were found black pumice stones, and salt kerned on the rocks, very white and glistering. This day also the master of the *Sunshine* took of the people a very strong lusty young fellow.

The 20 about two of the clock in the morning, the savages came to the island where our pinnace was built ready to be launched, and tore the two upper strakes, and carried them away only for the love of the iron in the boards. While they were about this practice, we manned the *Elizabeth's* boat to go ashore to them. Our men being either afraid or amazed, were so long before they came to shore, that our captain willed them to stay, and made the gunner give fire to a saker, and laid the piece level with the boat which the savages had turned on the one side, because we should not hurt them with our arrows ; and made the boat their bulwark against the arrows which we shot at them. Our gunner having made all things ready, gave fire to the piece, and fearing to hurt any of the people, and regarding the owner's profit, thought belike he would save a saker's shot, doubting we should have occasion to fight with men-of-war, and so shot off the saker without a bullet. We looking still when the savages that were hurt should run away without legs, at length we could perceive never a man hurt, but all having their legs could carry away their bodies. We had no sooner shot off the piece, but the master of the *Sunshine* manned his boat, and came rowing toward the island, the very sight of whom made each of them take that he had gotten, and flee away as fast as they could to another island about two miles off, where they took the nails out of the timber, and left the wood on the isle. When we came on shore, and saw how they had spoiled the boat, after much debating of the matter, we agreed that the *Elizabeth* should have her to fish withal: whereupon she was presently carried aboard, and stowed.

Now after this trouble, being resolved to depart with the first wind, there fell out another matter worse than all the rest, and that was in this manner. John Churchyard, one whom our captain had appointed as pilot in the pinnace, came to our captain, and Master Bruton, and told them that the good ship which we must all hazard our lives in, had three hundred strokes at one time as she rode in the harbour. This disquieted us all greatly, and many doubted to go in her. At length our captain, by whom we were all to be governed, determined rather to end his life with credit, than to return with infamy and disgrace, and so being all agreed, we purposed to live and die together, and committed ourselves to the ship. Now the 21, having brought all our things aboard, about eleven or twelve of the clock at night we set sail and departed from those isles, which lie in 64 degrees of latitude, our ships being all now at sea, and we shaping our course to go, coasting the land to the northwards upon the eastern shore, (which we called the shore of our merchants, because there we met with people which trafficked with us); but here we were not without doubt of our ship.

The 24 being in 67 degrees and 40 minutes, we had great store of whales, and a kind of sea-birds which the mariners call cortinous. This day about six of the clock at night, we espied two of the country people at sea, thinking at the first they had been two great seals, until we saw their oars glistering with the sun. They came rowing towards us, as fast as they could, and when they came within hearing, they held up their oars, and cried "Iliaout," making many signs ; and at last they came to us, giving us birds for bracelets, and of them I had a dart with a bone in it, or a piece of unicorn's horn, as I did judge. This dart he made store of, but when he saw a knife, he let it go, being more desirous of the knife than of his dart. These people continued rowing after our ship the space of three hours.

The 25 in the morning, at seven of the clock, we descried 30 savages rowing after us, being by judgment 10 leagues off from the shore. They brought us salmon peels, birds, and capelin, and we gave them pins, needles, bracelets, nails, knives, bells, looking-glasses, and other small trifles ; and for a knife, a nail or a bracelet (which they call ponigmah), they would sell their boat, coats, or anything they had, although they were far from the shore. We had but few skins of them, about 20, but they made signs to us that if we would go to the shore, we should have more store of chichsanege : they stayed with us till 11 of the clock, at which time we went to prayer, and they departed from us.

The 28 and 29 were foggy with clouds, the 30 day we took the height, and found ourselves in 72 degrees and 12 minutes of latitude both at noon and at night, the sun being 5 degrees above the horizon. At midnight the compass set to the variation of 28 degrees to the westward. Now having coasted the land, which we called London Coast, from the 21 of this present, till the 30, the sea open all to the westwards and northwards, the land on starboard side east from us, the wind shifted to the north, whereupon we left that shore, naming the same Hope Sanderson, and shaped our course west, and ran 40 leagues and better without the sight of any land.

July

The second of July we fell with a mighty bank of ice west from us, lying north and south, which bank we would gladly have doubled out to the northwards, but the wind would not suffer us, so that we were fain to coast it to the southwards, hoping to double it out, that we might have run so far west till we had found land, or else to have been thoroughly resolved of our pretended purpose.

The 3 we fell with the ice again, and putting off from it, we sought to the northwards, but the wind crossed us.

The 12 we coasted again the ice, having the wind at north-north-west. The 13 bearing off from the ice, we determined to go with the shore and come to an anchor, and to stay five or six days for the dissolving of the ice, hoping that the sea continually beating it, and the sun, with the extreme force of heat which it had, always shining upon it, would make a quick dispatch, that we might have a further search upon the western shore. Now when we were come to the

eastern coast, the water something deep, and some
of our company fearful withal, we durst not come
to an anchor, but bare off into the sea again. The
poor people seeing us go away again, came rowing
after us into the sea, the waves being somewhat
lofty.   We trucked with them for a few skins and
darts, and gave them beads, nails, pins, needles, and
cards, they pointing to the shore, as though they would
show us some great friendship : but we little regarding
their courtesy, gave them the gentle farewell, and so
departed.

The 19 at one o'clock after noon, we had sight of
the land which we called Mount Raleigh, and at 12 of
the clock at night, we were thwart the straits which
we discovered the first year. The 20 we traversed in
the mouth of the strait, the wind being at west, with
fair and clear weather. The 21 and 22 we coasted the
northern coast of the straits. The 23 having sailed
threescore leagues north-west into the straits, at two
o'clock after noon we anchored among many isles in
the bottom of the gulf, naming the same The Earl of
Cumberland's Isles, where riding at anchor, a whale
passed by our ship and went west in among the isles.
Here the compass set at 30 degrees westward variation.
The 23 we departed, shaping our course south-east to
recover the sea. The 25 we were becalmed in the
bottom of the gulf, the air being extreme hot   Master
Bruton and some of the mariners went on shore to
course dogs, where they found many graves, and train
spilt on the ground, the dogs being so fat that they
were scant able to run.

The 26 we had a pretty storm, the wind being at
south-east. The 27 and 28 were fair. The 29 we were

clear out of the straits, having coasted the south shore, and this day at noon we were in 62 degrees of latitude. The 30 in the afternoon we coasted a bank of ice, which lay on the shore, and passed by a great bank or inlet, which lay between 63 and 62 degrees of latitude, which we called Lumley's Inlet. We had oftentimes, as we sailed alongst the coast, great ruts, the water as it were whirling and overfalling, as if it were the fall of some great water through a bridge.

The 31 as we sailed by a headland, which we named Warwick's Foreland, we fell into one of those over-falls with a fresh gale of wind, and bearing all our sails, we looking upon an island of ice between us and the shore, had thought that our bark did make no way, which caused us to take marks on the shore. At length we perceived ourselves to go very fast, and the island of ice, which we saw before, was carried very forcibly with the set of the current faster than our ship went. This day and night we passed by a very great gulf, the water whirling and roaring as it were the meetings of tides.

August

The first of August having coasted a bank of ice which was driven out at the mouth of this gulf, we fell with the southermost cape of the gulf, which we named Chidley's Cape, which lay in 61 degrees and 10 minutes of latitude. The 12 we saw five deer on the top of an island, called by us Darcey's Island. And we hoised out our boat, and went ashore to them, thinking to have killed some of them. But when we came on shore, and had coursed them twice about the island, they took the sea and swam towards islands distant from that three leagues. When we perceived that they had taken the sea, we gave them over, because our boat was so small that it could not carry us, and row after them, they swam so fast : but one of them was as big as a good pretty cow, and very fat, their feet as big as ox feet. Here upon this island I killed with my piece a gray hare.

The 13 in the morning we saw three or four white bears, but durst not go on shore to them for lack of a good boat. This day we struck a rock seeking for an harbour, and received a leak : and this day we were in 54 degrees of latitude.

The 14 we stopped our leak in a storm not very outrageous, at noon.

The 15 being almost in 52 degrees of latitude, and not finding our ships, nor (according to their promise) any kind of mark, token, or beacon, which we willed them to set up, (and they protested to do so upon every headland, island, or cape, within twenty leagues every way off from their fishing place, which our captain appointed to be between 54 and 55 degrees), this 15, I say, we shaped our course homewards for England, having in our ship but little wood, and half a hogshead of fresh water. Our men were very willing to depart, and no man more forward than Pearson, for he feared to be put out of his office of stewardship ; but because every man was so willing to depart, we consented to return for our own country : and so we had the 16 fair weather, with the wind at south-west.

The 17 we met a ship at sea, and as far as we

could judge it was a Biscayan.   We thought she went
a-fishing for whales; for in 52 degrees or thereabout
we saw very many.

The 18 was fair, with a good gale at west.

The 19 fair also, with much wind at west and by
south.

And thus, after much variable weather and change
of winds, we arrived the 15 of September in Dartmouth, anno 1587, giving thanks to God for our safe
arrival.

HUDSON. LAST VOYAGE

(FOR THE DISCOVERY OF THE NORTH WEST PASSAGE) 1610

(BY ABACUK PRICKETT)[1]

[Sailing in one ship only, the *Discovery*, about the middle of April, 1610, they reached Greenland early in June, touching at Iceland on the way. From Greenland they sailed to the west, reached Hudson Strait towards the end of June, and entered Hudson Bay (called by Hudson "The Bay of God's Great Mercies") close to Cape Wolstenholme in the beginning of August. For three months they explored the southern part of the Bay, and there they were obliged to winter, the ship being frozen in by November 10. They had a scanty supply of provisions; there had already been signs of mutiny, and Hudson had displaced his mate Robert Juet and the boatswain Clement, appointing in their stead Robert Bylot (who became afterwards a well-known Arctic explorer) and William Wilson.]

---

[1] It should be borne in mind, in reading Prickett's narrative, with its hazy geographical details, that it was written with a view to whitewashing the mutineers, who had saved his life for this purpose, rather than to giving an account of the voyage. Dead men tell no tales, and so he throws part of the blame for the mutiny on Hudson himself, but the greater part on Greene and the others who had never returned. The survivors, including himself, are free from guilt.

We were victualled for six months in good proportion, and of that which was good: if our master would
have had more, he might have had it at home and in
other places. Here we were now, and therefore it
behoved us so to spend, that we might have (when

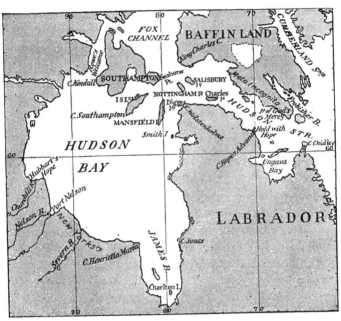

Hudson Bay and its approaches

time came) to bring us to the capes where the fowl
bred, for that was all the hope we had to bring us
home. Wherefore our master took order, first for
the spending of that we had, and then to increase it,
by propounding a reward to them that killed either
beast, fish, or fowl, as in his journal you have seen.

About the middle of this month of November, died John Williams, our gunner. God pardon the master's uncharitable dealing with this man. Now for that I am come to speak of him, out of whose ashes (as it were) that unhappy deed grew, which brought a scandal upon all that are returned home, and upon the action itself, the multitude (like the dog) running after the stone, but not at the caster: therefore, not to wrong the living nor slander the dead, I will (by the leave of God) deliver the truth as near as I can.

You shall understand that our master kept (in his house at London) a young man, named Henry Greene, born in Kent, of worshipful parents, but by his lewd life and conversation he had lost the good will of all his friends, and had spent all that he had. This man our master would have to sea with him, because he could write well. Our master gave him meat, and drink, and lodging, and by means of one Master Venson, with much ado got four pounds of his mother to buy him clothes, wherewith Master Venson would not trust him; but saw it laid out himself. This Henry Greene was not set down in the owners' book, nor any wages made for him. So Henry Greene stood upright, and very inward with the master, and was a serviceable man every way for manhood: but for religion he would say, he was clean paper, whereon he might write what he would. Now when our gunner was dead, and (as the order is in such cases) if the company stand in need of anything that belonged to the man deceased, then is it brought to the mainmast, and there sold to them that will give most for the same. This gunner had a gray cloth gown, which Greene prayed the master to friend him so much, as to let him

have it, paying for it as another would give. The master
saith he should, and thereupon he answered some.
that sought to have it, that Greene should have it,
and none else, and so it rested.

Now out of season and time the master calleth the
carpenter to go in hand with a house on shore, which
at the beginning our master would not hear, when it
might have been done. The carpenter told him, that
the snow and frost were such, as he neither could nor
would go in hand with such work. Which when our
master heard, he ferreted him out of his cabin to strike
him, calling him by many foul names, and threatening
to hang him. The carpenter told him that he knew
what belonged to his place better than himself, and
that he was no house carpenter. So this passed, and
the house was (after) made with much labour, but to
no end. The next day, after the master and the
carpenter fell out, the carpenter took his piece and
Henry Greene with him; for it was an order that none
should go out alone, but one with a piece, and another
with a pike. This did move the master so much the
more against Henry Greene. that Robert Bylot, his
mate, must have the gown, and had it delivered unto
him. Which when Henry Greene saw, he challenged
the master's promise; but the master did so rail on
Greene, with so many words of disgrace, telling him
that all his friends would not trust him with twenty
shillings, and therefore why should he? As for wages
he had none, nor none should have, if he did not please
him well. Yet the master had promised him to make
his wages as good as any man's in the ship; and to
have him one of the Prince's guard when we came
home. But you shall see how the devil out of this

so wrought with Greene, that he did the master what mischief he could, in seeking to discredit him, and to thrust him and many other honest men out of the ship in the end. To speak of all our trouble in this time of winter (which was so cold, as it lamed the most of our company, and myself do yet feel it) would be too tedious.

But I must not forget to shew how mercifully God dealt with us in this time. For the space of three months we had such store of fowl of one kind (which were partridges as white as milk), that we killed above an hundred dozen, besides others of sundry sorts: for all was fish that came to the net. The spring coming, this fowl left us: yet they were with us all the extreme cold. Then in their places came divers sort of other fowl, as swan, geese, duck, and teal, but hard to come by. Our master hoped they would have bred in those broken grounds, but they do not; but came from the south, and flew to the north, further than we were this voyage. Yet if they be taken short with the wind at north, or north-west, or north-east, then they fall and stay till the wind serve them, and then fly to the north. Now in time these fowls are gone, and few or none to be seen. Then we went into the woods, hills, and valleys, for all things that had any shew of substance in them, how vile soever: the moss of the ground, than the which I take the powder of a post to be much better, and the frog (in his engendering time as loathsome as a toad) was not spared. But amongst the divers sorts of buds, it pleased God that Thomas Woodhouse brought home a bud of a tree full of a turpentine substance. Of this our surgeon made a decoction to drink, and applied the buds hot to them that were troubled with ache in any part of their bodies; and for my part, I confess, I received great and present ease of my pain.

About this time, when the ice began to break out of the bays, there came a savage to our ship, as it were to see and to be seen, being the first that we had seen in all this time: whom our master entreated well, and made much of him, promising unto himself great matters by his means, and therefore would have all the knives and hatchets (which any man had) to his private use, but received none, but from John King, the carpenter, and myself. To this savage our master gave à knife, a looking-glass, and buttons, who received them thankfully, and made signs that after he had slept he would come again, which he did. When he came he brought with him a sled, which he drew after him, and upon it two deer skins and two beaver skins. He had a scrip under his arm, out of which he drew those things which the master had given him. He took the knife, and laid it upon one of the beaver skins, and his glasses and buttons upon the other, and so gave them to the master, who received them; and the savage took those things which the master had given him, and put them up into his scrip again. Then the master shewed him an hatchet, for which he would have given the master one of his deer skins, but our master would have them both, and so he had, although not willingly. After many signs of people to the north and to the south, and that after so many sleeps he would come again, he went his way, but never came more.

Now the ice being out of the sounds, so that our boat might go from one place unto another, a company

of men were appointed by the master to go a fishing
with our net. Their names were as followeth: William
Wilson, Henry Greene, Michael Perce, John Thomas,
Andrew Moter, Bennet Mathewes, and Arnold Lodlo.
These men, the first day they went, caught five hundred
fish, as big as good herrings, and some trouts. Which
put us all in some hope to have our wants supplied,
and our commons amended; but these were the most
that ever they got in one day, for many days they
got not a quarter so many. In this time of their
fishing, Henry Greene and William Wilson, with some
others, plotted to take the net and the shallop, which
the carpenter had now set up, and so to shift for
themselves. But the shallop being ready, our master
would go in it himself to the south and south-west,
to see if he could meet with the people; for to that
end was it set up, and (that way) we might see the
woods set on fire by them. So the master took the
seine and the shallop, and so much victual as would
serve for eight or nine days, and to the south he went.
They that remained aboard were to take in water,
wood, and ballast, and to have all things in a readiness
against he came back. But he set no time of his return,
for he was persuaded, if he could meet with the people,
he should have flesh of them, and that good store:
but he returned worse than he went forth. For he
could by no means meet with the people, although
they were near them, yet they would set the woods on
fire in his sight.

Being returned, he fitted all things for his return,
and first delivered all the bread out of the bread room
(which came to a pound a piece for every man's share),
and delivered also a bill of return, willing them to have

that to shew, if it pleased God that they came home:
and he wept when he gave it unto them. But to help
us in this poor estate with some relief, the boat and
seine went to work on Friday morning, and stayed
till Sunday noon: at which time they came aboard,
and brought fourscore small fish, a poor relief for so
many hungry bellies. Then we weighed and stood
out of our wintering place, and came to an anchor
without, in the mouth of the bay: from whence we
weighed and came to an anchor without in the sea,
where our bread being gone, that store of cheese we
had was to stop a gap, whereof there were five, whereat
the company grudged, because they made account of
nine. But those that were left were equally divided by
the master, although he had counsel to the contrary:
for there were some who having it, would make haste
to be rid thereof, because they could not govern it.
I knew when Henry Greene gave half his bread, which
he had for fourteen days, to one to keep, and prayed
him not to let him have any until the next Monday:
but before Wednesday at night he never left till he had
it again, having eaten up his first week's bread before.
So Wilson the boatswain hath eaten (in one day) his
fortnight's bread, and hath been two or three days
sick for his labour. The cause that moved the master
to deliver all the cheese, was because they were not
all of one goodness, and therefore they should see that
they had no wrong done them; but every man should
have alike the best and the worst together, which was
three pounds and a half for seven days.

The wind serving, we weighed and stood to the
north-west, and on Monday at night (the eighteenth
day of June) we fell into the ice, and the next day, the

wind being at west, we lay there till Sunday in sight of land. Now being here, the master told Nicholas Simmes that there would be a breaking up of chests and a search for bread, and willed him, if he had any, to bring it to him, which he did, and delivered to the master thirty cakes in a bag. This deed of the master (if it be true) hath made me marvel what should be the reason that he did not stop the breach in the beginning, but let it grow to that height, as that it overthrew himself and many other honest men: but "*there are many devices in the heart of man, yet the counsel of the Lord shall stand.*"

Being thus in the ice on Saturday, the one and twentieth of June, at night, Wilson the boatswain and Henry Greene came to me lying in my cabin lame, and told me that they and the rest of their associates would shift the company, and turn the master and all the sick men into the shallop, and let them shift for themselves. For there was not fourteen days' victual left for all the company, at that poor allowance they were at, and that there they lay, the master not caring to go one way or other: and that they had not eaten anything these three days, and therefore were resolute, either to mend or end, and what they had begun they would go through with it, or die. When I heard this, I told them I marvelled to hear so much from them, considering that they were married men, and had wives and children, and that for their sakes they should not commit so foul a thing in the sight of God and man, as that would be; for why should they banish themselves from their native country? Henry Greene bade me hold my peace, for he knew the worst, which was, to be hanged when he came home, and therefore

of the two he would rather be hanged at home than
starved abroad: and for the good will they bare me,
they would have me stay in the ship. I gave them
thanks, and told them that I came into her, not
to forsake her, yet not to hurt myself and others
by any such deed. Henry Greene told me then,
that I must take my fortune in the shallop. "If
there be no remedy," said I, "the will of God be
done."

Away went Henry Greene in a rage, swearing to
cut his throat that went about to disturb them, and
left Wilson by me, with whom I had some talk, but to
no good; for he was so persuaded, that there was no
remedy now but to go on while it was hot, lest their
party should fail them, and the mischief they had
intended to others should light on themselves. Henry
Greene came again, and demanded of him what I said.
Wilson answered: "He is in his old song, still patient."
Then I spake to Henry Greene to stay three days, in
which time I would so deal with the master that all
should be well. So I dealt with him to forbear but two
days, nay twelve hours. "There is no way," then say
they, "but out of hand." Then I told them, that if
they would stay till Monday, I would join with them to
share all the victuals in the ship, and would justify it
when I came home; but this would not serve their turns.
Wherefore I told them it was some worse matter they
had in hand, than they made show of, and that it was
blood and revenge he sought, or else he would not at such
a time of night undertake such a deed. Henry Greene
(with that) taketh my Bible which lay before me, and
sware that he would do no man harm, and what he
did was for the good of the voyage, and for nothing

else; and that all the rest should do the like. The like did Wilson swear.

Henry Greene went his way, and presently came Juet, who, because he was an ancient man, I hoped to have found some reason in him; but he was worse than Henry Greene, for he sware plainly that he would justify this deed when he came home. After him came John Thomas and Michael Perce, as birds of one feather; but because they are not living, I will let them go, as then I did. Then came Moter and Bennet, of whom I demanded, if they were well advised what they had taken in hand. They answered, they were, and therefore came to take their oath.

Now, because I am much condemned for this oath, as one of them that plotted with them, and that by an oath I should bind them together to perform what they had begun, I thought good here to set down to the view of all, how well their oath and deeds agreed: and thus it was:—"You shall swear truth to God, your prince and country: you shall do nothing, but to the glory of God, and the good of the action in hand, and harm to no man." This was the oath, without adding or diminishing. I looked for more of these companions (although these were too many), but there came no more. It was dark, and they in a readiness to put this deed of darkness in execution. I called to Henry Greene and Wilson, and prayed them not to go in hand with it in the dark, but to stay till the morning. Now, every man (I hoped) would go to his rest, but wickedness sleepeth not; for Henry Greene keepeth the master company all night (and gave me bread, which his cabin-mate gave him), and others are as watchful as he. Then I asked Henry Greene, whom he would put out with the master? He said, the carpenter, John King, and the sick men. I said, they should not do well to part with the carpenter, what need soever they should have. Why the carpenter was in no more regard amongst them was, first, for that he and John King were condemned for wrong done in the victual; but the chiefest cause was, for that the master loved him, and made him his mate upon his return out of our wintering place, thereby displacing Robert Bylot; whereat they did grudge, because he could neither write nor read. And therefore (said they) the master and his ignorant mate would carry the ship whither the master pleased: the master forbidding any man to keep account or reckoning, having taken from all men whatsoever served for that purpose. Well, I obtained of Henry Greene and Wilson that the carpenter should stay, by whose means I hoped (after they had satisfied themselves), that the master and the poor man might be taken into the ship again. Or, I hoped, that some one or other would give some notice, either to the carpenter, John King, or the master; for so it might have come to pass by some of them, that were the most forward.

Now, it shall not be amiss to show how we were lodged; and to begin in the cook room—there lay Bennet and the cooper lame: without the cook room, on the starboard side, lay Thomas Wydhouse sick; next to him lay Sidrack Funer lame; then the surgeon, and John Hudson with him; next to them lay Wilson the boatswain, and then Arnold Lodlo next to him: in the gun-room lay Robert Juet and John Thomas; on the larboard side lay Michael Bute and Adria Moore, who had never been well since we lost our anchor; next to them lay Michael Perce and Andrew Moter. Next to them, without the gun-room, lay John King, and with him Robert Bylot; next to them myself, and next to me Francis Clements. In the midship, between the capstan and the pumps, lay Henry Greene and Nicholas Simmes. This night John King was late up, and they thought he had been with the master; but he was with the carpenter, who lay on the poop, and coming down from him was met by his cabin-mate, as it were by chance, and so they came to their cabin together. It was not long ere it was day: then came Bennet for water for the kettle. He rose and went into the hold. When he was in, they shut the hatch on him (but who kept it down I know not); up upon the deck went Bennet.

In the meantime Henry Greene and another went to the carpenter, and held him with a talk, till the master came out of his cabin (which he soon did); then came John Thomas and Bennet before him, while Wilson bound his arms behind him. He asked them what they meant? They told him he should know, when he was in the shallop. Now Juet, while this was a doing, came to John King into the hold, who was provided for him, for he had got a sword of his own, and kept him at a bay, and might have killed him, but others came to help him: and so he came up to the master. The master called to the carpenter and told him that he was bound, but I heard no answer he made. Now Arnold Lodlo and Michael Bute railed at them, and told them their knavery would show itself. Then was the shallop haled up to the ship side, and the poor, sick, and lame men were called upon to get them out of their cabins into the shallop.

The master called to me, who came out of my cabin as well as I could to the hatchway, to speak with him ; where, on my knees I besought them, for the love of God, to remember themselves, and to do as they would be done unto. They bade me keep myself well, and get me into my cabin, not suffering the master to speak with me. But when I came into my cabin again, he called to me at the horn, which gave light into my cabin, and told me that Juet would over-throw us all. "Nay" (said I), "it is that villain Henry Greene," and I spake it not softly.

Now was the carpenter at liberty, who asked them if they would be hanged, when they came home : and as for himself, he said, he would not stay in the ship unless they would force him : they bade him go then, for they would not stay him. "I will" (said he), "so I may have my chest with me, and all that is in it." They said he should, and presently they put it into the shallop. Then he came down to me to take his leave of me, who persuaded him to stay ; which if he did he might so work that all should be well. He said he did not think, but they would be glad to take them in again. For he was so persuaded by the master, that there was not one in all the ship, that could tell how to carry her home. "But" (saith he), "if we must part, which we will not willingly do" (for they would follow the ship), he prayed me, if we came to the capes before them, that I would leave some token that we had been there, near to the place where the fowls bred, and he would do the like for us : and so (with tears) we parted. Now were the sick men driven out of their cabins into the shallop ; but John Thomas was Francis Clements's friend, and Bennet was the cooper's,

so as there were words between them and **Henry
Greene**, one saying that they should go, and the
other swearing that they should not go, but such
as were in the shallop should return.   When Henry
Greene heard that, he was compelled to give place, and
to put out Arnold Lodlo and Michael Bute, which
with much ado they did.

In the meantime, there were some of them that
plied their work, as if the ship had been entered by
force, and they had free leave to pillage, breaking up
chests and rifling all places.   One of them came by
me, who asked me what they should do.   I answered,
he should make an end of what he had begun ; for I
saw him do nothing but shark up and down.   Now
were all the poor men in the shallop, whose names are
as followeth : Henry Hudson, John Hudson, Arnold
Lodlo, Sidrack Funer, Phillip Staffe, Thomas Woodhouse or Wydhouse, Adam Moore, Henry King,
Michael Bute.   The carpenter got of them a piece,
and powder, and shot, and some pikes, an iron pot,
with some meal, and other things.   They stood out of
the ice, the shallop being fast to the stern of the ship,
and so (when they were nigh out, for I cannot say
they were clean out) they cut her head fast from the
stern of our ship, then out with their top-sails, and
towards the east they stood in a clear sea.   In the
end they took in their top-sails, righted their helm,
and lay under their foresail, till they had ransacked
and searched all places in the ship.   In the hold they
found one of the vessels of meal whole, and the other
half spent (for we had but two).   We found also two
firkins of butter, some twenty-seven pieces of pork,
half a bushel of peas ; but in the master's cabin we

found two hundred of biscuit cakes, a peck of meal, of beer to the quantity of a butt, one with another. Now it was said that the shallop was come within sight, they let fall the mainsail, and out with their top-sails, and fly as from an enemy.

Then I prayed them yet to remember themselves; but William Wilson (more than the rest) would hear of no such matter. Coming nigh the east shore they cast about, and stood to the west and came to an island, and anchored in sixteen or seventeen fathom water. So they sent the boat and the net ashore to see if they could have a draught; but could not for rocks and great stones. Michael Perce killed two fowl, and here they found good store of that weed, which we called cockle-grass in our wintering-place, whereof they gathered store, and came aboard again. Here we lay that night and the best part of the next day, in all which time we saw not the shallop, or ever after. Now Henry Greene came to me and told me, that it was the company's will, that I should come up into the master's cabin and take charge thereof. I told him it was more fit for Robert Juet: he said he should not come in it, nor meddle with the master's card or journals. So up I came, and Henry Greene gave me the key of the master's chest, and told me then that he had laid the master's best things together, which he would use himself, when time did serve: the bread was also delivered me by tale.

The wind serving, we stood to the north-east, and this was Robert Bylot's course, contrary to Robert Juet, who would have gone to the north-west. We had the eastern shore still in sight, and (in the night) had a stout gale of wind, and stood afore it till we

met with ice, into the which we ran from thin to thick,
till we could go no further for ice, which lay so thick
ahead of us (and the wind brought it after us astern),
that we could not stir backward nor forward; but so
lay embayed fourteen days in worse ice than ever we
met to deal withal, for we had been where there was
greater store, but it was not so broad upon the water
as this; for this floating ice contained miles and half
miles in compass, where we had a deep sea, and a tide
of flood and ebb, which set north-west and south-east.
Here Robert Juet would have gone to the north-west,
but Robert Bylot was confident to go through to the
north-east, which he did. At last, being clear of this ice,
he continued his course in sight of the eastern shore till
he raised four islands, which lay north and south; but
we passed them six or seven leagues, the wind took us
so short. Then we stood back to them again, and
came to an anchor between two of the most norther-
most. We sent the boat ashore, to see if there were
anything there to be had, but found nothing but
cockle-grass, whereof they gathered store, and so
returned aboard. Before we came to this place, I
might well see that I was kept in the ship against
Henry Greene's mind, because I did not favour their
proceedings better than I did. Then he began (very
subtly) to draw me to take upon me to search for
those things, which himself had stolen: and accused
me of a matter no less than treason amongst us, that
I had deceived the company of thirty cakes of bread.
Now they began to talk amongst themselves, that
England was no safe place for them, and Henry Greene
swore the ship should not come into any place (but
keep the sea still), till he had the King's Majesty's hand

and seal to show for his safety. They had many devices in their heads, but Henry Greene in the end was their captain, and so called of them.

From these islands we stood to the north-east and the easter land still in sight: we raised those islands, that our master called Rumney's Islands. Between these islands and the shallow ground to the east of them, our master went down into the first great bay. We kept the east shore still in our sight, and coming thwart of the low land, we ran on a rock that lay under water, and struck but once; for if she had, we might have been made inhabitants of that place; but God sent us soon off without any harm that we saw. We continued our course and raised land ahead of us, which stretched out to the north. Which when they saw, they said plainly that Robert Bylot by his northerly course had left the capes to the south, and that they were best to seek down to the south in time for relief, before all was gone; for we had small store left. But Robert Bylot would follow the land to the north, saying that he hoped in God to find somewhat to relieve us that way, as soon as to the south. I told them that this land was the main of Wolstenholme Cape, and that the shallow rocky ground was the same that the master went down by, when he went into the great bay. Robert Juet and all said it was not possible, unless the master had brought the ship over land, and willed them to look into the master's card and their course, how well they did agree. We stood to the east and left the mainland to the north, by many small islands into a narrow gut between two lands, and there came to an anchor. The boat went ashore on the north side, where we found the great horn, but nothing

else. The next day we went to the south side, but
found nothing there save cockle-grass, of which we
gathered. This grass was a great relief unto us, for
without it we should hardly have got to the capes
for want of victual. The wind serving, we stood out,
but before we could get clean out, the wind came to
the west, so that we were constrained to anchor on
the north side.

The next day we weighed and doubled the point
of the north land, which is high land, and so continued to the capes, lying north and south, some five-
and-twenty or thirty leagues. To the north we stood,
to see store of those fowls, that breed in the capes, and
to kill some with our shot, and to fetch them with our
boat. We raised the capes with joy and bare for them,
and came to the islands that lie in the mouth of the
strait; but bearing in between the rocky isles, we
ran on a rock that lay under water, and there stuck
fast eight or nine hours. It was ebbing water when
we thus came on, so the flood set us afloat, God guiding
both wind and sea, that it was calm and fair weather:
the ebb came from the east, and the flood from the
west. When we were afloat we stood more near to
the east shore, and there anchored.

The next day, being the seven and twentieth of
July, we sent the boat to fetch some fowl, and the ship
should weigh and stand as near as they could; for the
wind was against us. They had a great way to row,
and by that means they could not reach to the place
where the fowl bred; but found good store of gulls,
yet hard to come by, on the rocks and cliffs; but with
their pieces they killed some thirty, and towards night
returned. Now we had brought our ship more near

to the mouth of the straits, and there came to an anchor in eighteen or twenty fathom water, upon a reef or shelf of ground. Which after they had weighed their anchor, and stood more near to the place where the fowl bred, they could not find it again, nor no place like it: but were fain to turn to and fro in the mouth of the strait, and to be in danger of rocks, because they could not find ground to let fall an anchor in, the water was so deep.

The eight and twentieth day, the boat went to Digges's Cape for fowl, and made directly for the place where the fowl bred, and being near, they saw seven boats come about the eastern point towards them. When the savages saw our boat, they drew themselves together, and drew their lesser boats into their bigger: and when they had done, they came rowing to our boat, and made signs to the west, but they made ready for all assays. The savages came to them, and by signs grew familiar one with another, so as our men took one of theirs into our boat, and they took one of ours into their boat. Then they carried our man to a cove where their tents stood, toward the west of the place where the fowl bred: so they carried him into their tents, where he remained till our men returned with theirs. Our boat went to the place where the fowl bred, and were desirous to know how the savages killed their fowl. He showed them the manner how, which was thus: they take a long pole with a snare at the end, which they put about the fowl's neck, and so pluck them down. When our men knew that they had a better way of their own, they showed him the use of our pieces, which at one shot would kill seven or eight. To be short, our boat returned to their cove for our man and to deliver theirs. When they came, they made great joy, with dancing, and leaping, and stroking of their breasts: they offered divers things to our men, but they only took some morses' teeth, which they gave them for a knife and two glass buttons: and so, receiving our man, they came aboard, much rejoicing at this chance, as if they had met with the most simple and kind people of the world.

And Henry Greene (more than the rest) was so confident, that by no means we should take care to stand on our guard: God blinding him so, that where he made reckoning to receive great matters from these people, he received more than he looked for, and that suddenly, by being made a good example for all men, that make no conscience of doing evil; and that we take heed of the savage people, how simple soever they seem to be.

The next day, the nine and twentieth of July, they made haste to be ashore, and because the ship rid too far off, they weighed and stood as near to the place where the fowl bred, as they could; and because I was lame, I was to go in the boat, to carry such things as I had in the cabin, of everything somewhat; and so, with more haste than good speed (and not without swearing), away we went, Henry Greene, William Wilson, John Thomas, Michael Perce, Andrew Moter, and myself. When we came near the shore, the people were on the hills dancing and leaping: to the cove we came, where they had drawn up their boats: we brought our boat to the east side of the cove, close to the rocks. Ashore they went, and made fast the boat to a great stone on the shore. The people came, and every one had somewhat in his hand to barter; but Henry Greene swore they should have nothing till he had venison, for that they had so promised him by signs.

Now when we came, they made signs to their dogs (whereof there were many like mongrels, as big as hounds), and pointed to their mountain and to the sun, clapping their hands. Then Henry Greene, John Thomas, and William Wilson stood hard by the boat head; Michael Perce and Andrew Moter were got up upon the rock a gathering of sorrel. Not one of them had any weapon about him, not so much as a stick, save Henry Greene only, who had a piece of a pike in his hand: nor saw I anything, that they had, wherewith to hurt us. Henry Greene and William Wilson had looking-glasses, and Jews' trumps, and bells, which they were showing the people. The savages standing round about them, one of them came into the boat's head to me to show me a bottle: I made signs to him to get him ashore, but he made as though he had not understood me, whereupon I stood up and pointed him ashore. In the meantime another stole behind me to the stern of the boat, and when I saw him ashore, that was in the head of the boat, I sat down again; but suddenly I saw the leg and foot of a man by me. Wherefore I cast up my head, and saw the savage with his knife in his hand, who struck at my breast over my head: I cast up my right arm to save my breast; he wounded my arm, and struck me into the body under my right pap. He struck a second blow, which I met with my left hand, and then he struck me into the right thigh, and had like to have cut off my little finger of the left hand. Now I had got hold of the string of the knife, and had wound it about my left hand, he striving with both his hands to make an end of that he had begun : I found him but weak in the grip (God enabling me), and getting hold of the sleeve of his left arm, so bare him from me.   His left side lay bare to me, which when I saw, I put his sleeve off his left arm into my left hand, holding the string of the knife fast in the same hand; and having got my right hand at liberty, I sought for somewhat wherewith to strike him (not remembering my dagger at my side), but looking down I saw it, and therewith struck him into the body and the throat.

Whiles I was thus assaulted in the boat, our men were set upon on the shore.   John Thomas and William Wilson had their bowels cut, and Michael Perce and Henry Greene, being mortally wounded, came tumbling into the boat together.   When Andrew Moter saw this medley, he came running down the rocks, and leaped into the sea, and so swam to the boat, hanging on the stern thereof, till Michael Perce took him in, who manfully made good the head of the boat against the savages, that pressed sore upon us.   Now Michael Perce had got an hatchet, wherewith I saw him strike one of them, that he lay sprawling in the sea.   Henry Greene crieth " *Coragio*," and layeth about him with his truncheon.   I cried to them to clear the boat, and Andrew Moter cried to be taken in.   The savages betook them to their bows and arrows, which they sent amongst us, wherewith Henry Greene was slain outright, and Michael Perce received many wounds, and so did the rest.   Michael Perce cleareth the boat, and puts it from the shore, and helpeth Andrew Moter in; but in turning of the boat I received a cruel wound in my back with an arrow. Michael Perce and Andrew Moter rowed the boat away; which when the savages saw, they ran to their boats, and I feared they would have launched them to have followed us, but they did not, and our ship was in the middle of the channel and could not see us.

Now when they had rowed a good way from the shore, Michael Perce fainted, and could row no more. Then was Andrew Moter driven to stand in the boat head, and waft to the ship, which at the first saw us not, and when they did, they could not tell what to make of us; but in the end they stood for us, and so took us up. Henry Greene was thrown out of the boat into the sea, and the rest were had aboard, the savage being yet alive, yet without sense. But they died all there that day, William Wilson swearing and cursing in most fearful manner. Michael Perce lived two days after, and then died. Thus you have heard the tragical end of Henry Greene and his mates, whom they called captain, these four being the only lusty men in all the ship.

The poor number, that was left, were to ply our ship to and fro in the mouth of the strait; for there was no place to anchor in near hand. Besides, they were to go in the boat to kill fowl to bring us home, which they did, although with danger to us all. For if the wind blew, there was an high sea, and the eddies of the tides would carry the ship so near the rocks, as it feared our master, for so I will now call him. After they had killed some two hundred fowl, with great labour, on the south cape, we stood to the east; but when we were six or seven leagues from the capes, the wind came up at east. Then we stood back to the

capes again, and killed an hundred fowl more. After
this the wind came to the west, so we were driven to
go away, and then our master stood (for the most)
along by the north shore, till he fell into broken ground
about the Queen's Foreland, and there anchored.
From thence we went to God's Mercies, and from thence
to those islands, which lie in the mouth of our strait,
not seeing the land till we were ready to run our bow-
sprit against the rocks in a fog. But it cleared a little,
and then we might see ourselves enclosed with rocky
islands, and could find no ground to anchor in. There
our master lay a-try all night, and the next day, the
fog continuing, they sought for ground to anchor in,
and found some in an hundred and odd fathoms of
water. The next day we weighed and stood to the
east, but before we came here, we had put ourselves
to hard allowance, as half a fowl a day with the pottage;
for yet we had some meal left, and nothing else. Then
they began to make trial of all whatsoever. We had
flayed our fowl, for they will not pull; and Robert
Juet was the first that made use of the skins by burning
of the feathers: so they became a great dish of meat,
and as for the garbage, it was not thrown away.

After we were clear of these islands, which lie out
with two points, one to the south-east and the other
to the north, making a bay to the sight, as if there
were no way through, we continued our course east-
south-east and south and by east, to raise the Desolations, from thence to shape our course for Ireland.
Thus we continued divers days; but the wind, coming
against us, made us to alter our course, and by the means
of Robert Juet, who persuaded the company that
they should find great relief in Newfoundland, if our

countrymen were there, and if they were gone before we came, yet should we find great store of bread and fish left ashore by them; but how true, I give God thanks we did not try. Yet we stood to the south-west and to the west, almost to fifty-seven degrees; when (by the will of God) the wind came up at south-west. Then the master asked me, if he should take the benefit of this wind, and shape his course for Ireland. I said it was best to go, where we knew corn grew, and not to seek it, where it was cast away and not to be found. Towards Ireland now we stood, with prosperous winds for many days together. Then was all our meal spent, and our fowl reasty and dry; but (being no remedy) we were content with the salt broth for dinner and the half fowl for supper. Now went our candles to wrack, and Bennet, our cook, made a mess of meat of the bones of the fowl, frying them with candle grease till they were crisp, and, with vinegar put to them, made a good dish of meat. Our vinegar was shared, and to every man a pound of candles delivered for a week, as a great dainty. Now Robert Juet (by his reckoning) saith we were within sixty or seventy leagues of Ireland, when we had two hundred thither. And sure our course was so much the longer through our evil steerage; for our men became so weak, that they could not stand at the helm, but were fain to sit.

Then Robert Juet died for mere want, and all our men were in despair, and said we were past Ireland, and our last fowl were in the steep-tub. So our men cared not which end went forward, insomuch as our master was driven to look to their labour, as well as his own; for some of them would sit and see the fore-sail or mainsail fly up to the tops, the sheets being

either flown or broken, and would not help it themselves, nor call to others for help, which much grieved
the master. Now in this extremity it pleased God
to give us sight of land, not far from the place our
master said he would fall withal, which was the
bay of Galway, and we fell to the west of the Durseys,
and so stood along by the coast to the south-west. In
the end there was a joyful cry, "A sail, a sail," towards
which they stood. Then they saw more, but to the
nearest we stood, and called to him; his bark was of
Fowey, and was at anchor a fishing. He came to us,
and brought us into Bere Haven. From Bere Haven
we came to Plymouth, and so to an anchor before the
castle; and from Plymouth, with fair wind and weather,
without stop or stay we came to the Downs; from
thence to Gravesend, where most of our men went
ashore, and from thence came on this side Erith, and
there stopped. Where our master Robert Bylot came
aboard, and so had me up to London with him, and so
we came to Sir Thomas Smith's together.

William Barents

Reproduced, by kind permission of the publisher, from Dr A D. de Vries's *Oud-Holland* (Binger, 1882). Originally a vignette in a chart published in Amsterdam between 1613 and 1615.

WILLIAM BARENTS

The Third Voyage northward to the Kingdoms of Cathaia and China, in anno 1596

(By Gerrit de Veer)

In the beginning of this year, there was two ships rigged and set forth by the town of Amsterdam, to sail that voyage. In the one, Jacob Heemskerck Hendrickson was master and factor for the wares and merchandise, and William Barents chief pilot. In the other, John Cornelison Rijp was both master and factor for the goods, that the merchants had laden in her.

The 5 of May all the men in both the ships were mustered, and upon the tenth of May they sailed from Amsterdam.

The first of June we had no night, and the second of June we had the wind contrary; but upon the fourth of June we had a good wind out of the west-north-west, and sailed north-east.

And when the sun was about south-south-east (half-past 9 a.m.), we saw a strange sight in the element: for on each side of the sun there was another sun, and two rainbows that passed clean through the three suns, and then two rainbows more, the one compassing round about the suns, and the other cross through the great

roundel; the great roundel standing with the uttermost
point elevated above the horizon 28 degrees.

The fifth of June we saw the first ice, which we
wondered at, at the first thinking that it had been
white swans; for one of our men walking in the fore-
deck on a sudden began to cry out with a loud voice,
and said that he saw white swans: which we that were

A wonder in the heavens, and how we caught a bear

under hatches hearing, presently came up, and perceived
that it was ice, that came driving from the great heap,
showing like swans, it being then about evening.

The ninth of June we found the island, that lay
under 74 degrees and 30 minutes.

The 12 of June, in the morning, we saw a white
bear, which we rowed after with our boat, thinking to

cast a rope about her neck; but when we were near her, she was so great that we durst not do it, but rowed back again to our ship, to fetch more men and our arms, and so made to her again with muskets, arquebuses, halberts, and hatchets, John Cornelison's men coming also with their boat to help us. And so being well furnished of men and weapons, we rowed with both our boats unto the bear, and fought with her, while four glasses were run out, for our weapons could do her little hurt; and amongst the rest of the blows that we gave her, one of our men struck her into the back with an axe, which stuck fast in her back, and yet she swam away with it; but we rowed after her, and at last we cut her head in sunder with an axe, wherewith she died. And then we brought her into John Cornelison's ship, where we flayed her, and found her skin to be twelve foot long. Which done, we ate some of her flesh; but we brooked it not well. This island we called the Bear Island.

The 13 of June we left the island, and sailed north and somewhat easterly.

The 19 of June we saw land again. This land was very great, and we sailed westward along by it.

The 21 of June we cast out our anchor at 18 fathom before the land; and then we and John Cornelison's men rode on the west side of the land, and there fetched ballast: and when we got on board again with our ballast, we saw a white bear, that swam towards our ship. Whereupon we left off our work, and entering into the boat with John Cornelison's men, rowed after her, and crossing her in the way, drove her from the land; wherewith she swam further into the sea, and we followed her. And for that our

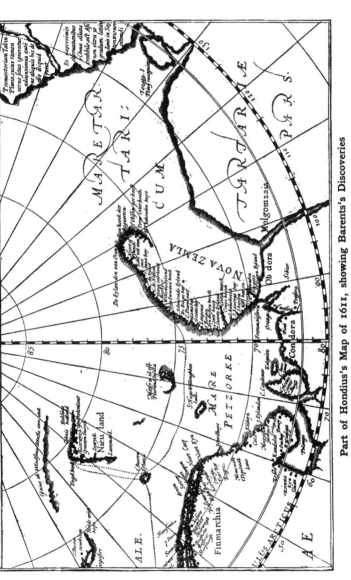

Part of Hondius's Map of 1611, showing Barents's Discoveries

boat could not make way after her, we manned out
our scute also, the better to follow her: but she swam
four miles into the sea; yet we followed her with the
most part of all our men of both ships in three boats,
and struck oftentimes at her, cutting and hewing her,
so that all our arms were most broken in pieces. During
our fight with her, she struck her claws so hard in our

How a bear came unto our boat, and what took place with him

boat, that the signs thereof were seen in it; but as
hap was, it was in the forehead of our boat: for if it
had been in the middle thereof, she had (peradventure)
overthrown it, they have such force in their claws. At
last, after we had fought long with her, and made her
weary with our three boats, that kept about her, we
overcame her, and killed her: which done, we brought

her into our ship, and flayed her, her skin being 13 foot long.

After that, we rowed with our scute about four miles inward to the land, where there was a good haven and good anchor ground, on the east side being sandy. There we cast out our lead, and found 16 fathom deep, and after that 10 and 12 fathom; and rowing further, we found that on the east side there was two islands, that reached eastward into the sea: on the west side also there was a great creek or river, which shewed also like an island. Then we rowed to the island, that lay in the middle, and there we found many brent geese, which we saw sitting upon their nests, and drave them from them, and they flying away cried: "Rot, rot, rot." And as they sat, we killed one goose dead with a stone, which we dressed and ate, and at least 60 eggs, that we took with us aboard the ship; and upon the 22 of June we went aboard our ship again.

Those geese were true brent geese, such as come into Holland about Wieringen, and every year are there taken in abundance, but till this time it was never known, where they laid and hatched their eggs; so that some men have taken upon them to write that they grow upon trees in Scotland, that hang over the water, and the fruits, which fall from them down into the water, become young geese and swim away; but those, that fall upon the land, burst in sunder and are lost. But this is now found to be contrary, and it is not to be wondered at, that no man could tell where they breed their eggs, for that no man, that ever we knew, had ever been under 80 degrees, nor that land under 80 degrees was never set down in any card, much less the brent geese that breed therein.

The first of July we saw the Bear Island again, and
then John Cornelison and his officers came aboard of
our ship, to speak with us about altering of our course;
but we being of a contrary opinion, it was agreed that
we should follow on our course, and he his: which was,
that he (according to his desire) should sail unto 80
degrees again; for he was of opinion, that there he
should find a passage through, on the east side of the
land, that lay under 80 degrees.   And upon that agree-
ment we left each other, they sailing northward, and
we southward because of the ice, the wind being east-
south-east.

The second of July we sailed eastward, and on
the 17 we saw the land of Nova Zembla.   Then we
altered our course, and sailed north-east and by north,
and on the 19 we came to the Cross Island.   There
stood two crosses upon the land, whereof it had the
name.

The twentieth of July we anchored under the island,
for we could get no further for the ice.   There we put
out our boat, and with eight men rowed on land, and
went to one of the crosses, where we rested us awhile,
to go to the next cross; but being in the way we saw
two bears by the other cross, at which time we had no
weapons at all about us.   The bears rose up upon their
hinder feet to see us (for they smell further than they
see), and for that they smelt us, therefore they rose
upright and came towards us, wherewith we were not
a little abashed, in such sort that we had little lust to
laugh, and in all haste went to our boat again, still
looking behind us to see if they followed us, thinking
to get into the boat, and so put off from the land: but
the master stayed us, saying, "He that first begins to

run away, I will thrust this boat-hook" (which he
then held in his hand) "into his ribs, for it is better
for us" (said he), "to stay all together, and see if we
can make them afraid with whooping and holloaing."
And so we went softly towards the boat, and got away

Map of Novaya Zemlya, showing entrances to Kara Sea

glad that we had escaped their claws, and that we
had the leisure to tell our fellows thereof.

The 5 of August we set sail again towards Ice
Point, and on the 7 we had a west-south-west wind,
and sailed along by the land, south-east and south-east

and by east, and saw but a little ice, and then passed by Cape Comfort, which we had much longed for.

The 16 of August ten of our men entering into one boat, rowed to the firm land at Nova Zembla, and drew the boat up upon the ice; which done, we went up a high hill to see the situation of the land, and found that it reached south-east and south-south-east, and then again south, which we disliked, for that it lay so much southward: but when we saw open water south-east and east-south-east, we were much comforted again, thinking that we had won our voyage, and knew not how we should get soon enough on board, to certify William Barents thereof.

The 19 of August it was indifferent good weather, the wind blowing south-west, the ice still driving, and we set sail with an indifferent gale of wind, and passed by Cape Desire, whereby we were once again in good hope.

The 26 of August there blew a reasonable gale of wind, at which time we determined to sail back to Cape Desire, and so home again, seeing that we could not get through by the way towards the Weygats, although we used all the means and industry we could, to get forward; but when we had passed by the Ice Haven, the ice began to drive with such force, that we were enclosed round about therewith, and yet we sought all the means we could to get out, but it was all in vain. And at that time we had like to have lost three men, that were upon the ice to make way for the ship, if the ice had held the course it went; but as we drove back again, and that the ice also, whereon our men stood, in like sort drove, they being nimble, as the ship drove by them, one of them caught hold of

the beak head, another upon the shrouds, and the
third upon the great brace that hung out behind, and
so by great adventure, by the hold that they took, they
got safe into the ship again, for which they thanked
God with all their hearts: for it was much likelier
that they should rather have been carried away with
the ice, but God, by the nimbleness of their hands,

How our ship stuck fast in the ice, whereby three of us were
nearly lost

delivered them out of that danger, which was a pitiful
thing to behold, although it fell out for the best,
for if they had not been nimble, they had surely died
for it.

The same day in the evening we got to the west
side of the Ice Haven, where we were forced, in great

cold, poverty, misery, and grief, to stay all that winter; the wind being then east north-east.

The 27 of August the ice drove round about the ship, and yet it was good weather; at which time we went on land, and being there, it began to blow south-east with a reasonable gale, and then the ice came with great force before the bow, and drove the ship up four

How the ice heaved up the fore part of our ship

foot high before, and behind it seemed as if the keel lay on the ground, so that it seemed that the ship would be overthrown in the place. Whereupon they that were in the ship put out the boat, therewith to save their lives, and withal put out a flag, to make a sign to us to come on board: which we perceiving, and beholding the ship to be lifted up in that sort, made all the haste we could to get on board, thinking that the ship was burst in pieces, but coming unto it, we found it to be in better case, than we thought it had been.

The 28 of August we got some of the ice from it, and the ship began to sit upright again; but before it was fully upright, as William Barents and the other pilot went forward to the bow, to see how the ship lay, and how much it was risen, and while they were busy upon their knees and elbows to measure how much it was, the ship burst out of the ice with such a noise and so great a crack, that they thought verily that they were all cast away, knowing not how to save themselves.

The 29 of August, the ship lying upright again, we used all the means we could, with iron crowbars and other instruments, to break the flakes of ice that lay one heaped upon the other, but all in vain; so that we determined to commit ourselves to the mercy of God, and to attend aid from him, for that the ice drove not away in any such sort, that it could help us.

The 30 of August the ice began to drive together one upon the other with greater force than before, and bare against the ship with a boisterous south-west wind and a great snow, so that all the whole ship was borne up and enclosed, whereby all that was both about and in it began to crack, so that it seemed to burst in a hundred pieces, which was most fearful both to see and hear, and made all the hair of our heads to rise upright with fear; and after that, the ship (by the ice on both sides, that joined and got under the same) was driven so upright, in such sort as if it had been lifted up with a wrench or vice.

The 5 of September it was fair sunshine weather and very calm; and at evening, when we had supped, the ice compassed about us again, and we were hard enclosed therewith, the ship beginning to lie upon the one side and suffered much, but by God's grace it still remained tight, wherewith we were wholly in fear to lose the ship, it was in so great danger. At which time we took counsel together, and carried our old foresail, with powder, lead, pieces, muskets, and other furniture on land, to make a tent or hut about our scute, that we had drawn upon the land; and at that time we carried some bread and wine on land also, with some carpenter's tools, therewith to mend our boat, that it might serve us in time of need.

The 6 of September it was indifferent fair sea-weather and sunshine, the wind being west, whereby we were somewhat comforted, hoping that the ice would drive away, and that we might get from thence again.

The 7 of September it was indifferent weather again, but we perceived no opening of the water, but to the contrary we lay hard enclosed with ice, and no water at all about the ship, no, not so much as a bucket-ful. The same day five of our men went on land, but two of them came back again; the other three went forward about eight miles into the land, and there found a river of sweet water, where also they found great store of wood, that had been driven thither, and there they found the footsteps of harts and hinds, as they thought, for they were cloven footed, some greater footed than others, which made them judge them to be so.

The 11 of September it was calm weather, and

eight of us went on land, every man armed, to see if
that were true, as our other three companions had said,
that there lay wood about the river; for that seeing
we had so long wound and turned about, sometime in
the ice and then again got out, and thereby were
compelled to alter our course, and at last saw that we
could not get out of the ice, but rather became faster,
and could not loose our ship as at other times we had
done, as also that it began to be near autumn and
winter, we took counsel together what we were best to
do according to the time, that we might winter there
and attend such adventure as God would send us. And
after we had debated upon the matter, to keep and
defend ourselves both from the cold and the wild beasts,
we determined to build a shed or house upon the land,
to keep us therein as well as we could, and so to commit
ourselves unto the tuition of God. And to that end we
went further into the land, to find out the convenientest
place in our opinions to raise our house upon, and yet
we had not much stuff to make it withal, in regard
that there grew no trees, nor any other thing in that
country convenient to build it withal. But we leaving
no occasion unsought, as our men went abroad to
view the country, and to see what good fortune might
happen unto us, at last we found an unexpected
comfort in our need, which was that we found certain
trees, roots and all, (as our three companions had said
before), which had been driven upon the shore, either
from Tartaria, Muscovia, or elsewhere; for there was
none growing upon that land. Wherewith (as if God
had purposely sent them unto us) we were much comforted, being in good hope that God would show us
some further favour; for that wood served us not

only to build our house, but also to burn and serve us all the winter long; otherwise without all doubt we had died there miserably with extreme cold.

The 15 of September, in the morning, as one of our men held watch, we saw three bears, whereof the one lay still behind a piece of ice, and the other two came close to the ship, which we perceiving, made our pieces ready to shoot at them; at which time there stood a tub full of meat upon the ice, which lay upon the ice, to freshen, for that close by the ship there was no water.   One of the bears went unto it, and put in his head to take out a piece of the meat, but she fared therewith as the dog did with the pudding; for as she was snatching at the beef she was shot into the head, wherewith she fell down dead and never stirred. The other bear stood still, and looked upon her fellow; and when she had stood a good while, she smelt her fellow, and perceiving that she was dead, she ran away, but we took halberts and other arms with us and followed her.   And at last she came again towards us, and we prepared ourselves to withstand her, wherewith she rose up upon her hinder feet, thinking to ramp at us; but while she reared herself up, one of our men shot her into the belly, and with that she fell upon her fore-feet again, and roaring as loud as she could, ran away.

The 17 of September thirteen of us went where the wood lay with our sleds, and so drew five and five in a sled, and the other three helped to lift the wood behind, to make us draw the better and with more ease; and in that manner we drew wood twice a day, and laid it on a heap by the place where we meant to build our house

The 25 of September we raised up the principals of our house, and began to work hard thereon.

The 26 of September we had a west wind and an open sea, but our ship lay fast, wherewith we were not a little grieved; but it was God's will, which we must patiently bear, and we began to make up our house: part of our men fetched wood to burn, the

How we built a house of wood, wherein to keep ourselves through the winter

rest played the carpenters and were busy about the house. As then we were sixteen men in all, for our carpenter was dead, and of our sixteen men there was still one or other sick.

The 27th of September it blew hard north-east, and it froze so hard that, as we put a nail into our mouths (as, when men work carpenters' work, they use to do), there would ice hang thereon when we took it out again, and make the blood follow. The same day there came an old bear and a young one towards us as we were going to our house, being all together (for we durst not go alone), which we thought to shoot at, but she ran away.

The 29 of September, in the morning, the wind was west, and after noon it blew east, and then we saw three bears between us and the house, an old one and two young; but we notwithstanding drew our goods from the ship to the house, and so got before the bears, and yet they followed us. Nevertheless we would not shun the way for them, but holloaed out as loud as we could, thinking that they would have gone away; but they would not once go out of their footpath, but got before us, wherewith we and they that were at the house made a great noise, which made the bears run away, and we were not a little glad thereof.

The 5 of October we brake up the lower deck of the fore-part of our ship, and with those deals we covered our house, and made it slope overhead that the water might run off.

The 8 of October, all the night before it blew so hard and the same day also, and snowed so fast that we should have smothered, if we had gone out into the air; and to speak truth, it had not been possible for any man to have gone one ship's length, though his life had lain thereon; for it was not possible for us to go out of the house or ship.

The 11 of October it was calm weather, the wind being south and somewhat warm, and then we carried our wine and other victuals on land; and as we were hoising the wine overboard, there came a bear towards our ship that had lain behind a piece of ice, and it seemed that we had waked her with the noise we made; for we had seen her lie there, but we thought her to be a piece of ice; but as she came near us, we shot at her, and she ran away, so we proceeded in our work.

The 12 of October it blew north and somewhat westerly, and then half of our men slept in the house, and that was the first time that we lay in it; but we endured great cold because our cabins were not made, and besides that we had not clothes enough, and we could keep no fire, because our chimney was not made, whereby it smoked exceedingly.

The 19 of October the wind blew north-east, and then there was but two men and a boy in the ship, at which time there came a bear that sought forcibly to get into the ship, although the two men shot at her with pieces of wood, and yet she ventured upon them, whereby they were in an extreme fear; and each of them seeking to save themselves, the two men leapt into the hold, and the boy climbed up the fore-rigging to save their lives. Meantime some of our men shot at her with a musket, and then she ran away.

The 20 of October it was calm sunshine weather, and then again we saw some open places of water in the sea, at which time we went on board to fetch the rest of our beer out of the ship, where we found some of the barrels frozen in pieces, and the iron hoops that were upon the spruce-beer barrels were also frozen in pieces.

The 21 of October it was calm sunshine weather, and then we had almost fetched all our victuals out of the ship.

The 24 of October we drew our boat home to our house, and turned the bottom thereof upwards, that, when time served us (if God saved our lives in the winter time), we might use it. And after that, perceiving that the ship lay fast and that there was nothing less to be expected than the opening of the water, we put our anchor into the ship again, because it should not be covered over and lost in the snow, that in the spring time we might use it : for we always trusted in God that he would deliver us from thence towards summer time either one way or other.

Things standing at this point with us, as the sun (when we might see it best and highest) began to be very low, we used all the speed we could to fetch all things with sleds out of our ship into our house, not only meat and drink, but all other necessaries ; at which time the wind was north.

The 26 of October we fetched all things that were necessary for the furnishing of our scute and our boat ; and when we had laden the last sled, and stood ready to draw it to the house, our master looked about him and saw three bears behind the ship, that were coming towards us, whereupon he cried out aloud to fear them away, and we presently leaped forth to defend ourselves as well as we could. And as good fortune was, there lay two halberds upon the sled, whereof the master took one, and I the other, and made resistance against them as well as we could ; but the rest of our men ran to save themselves in the ship, and as they ran, one of them fell into a cleft of ice, which grieved us much, for we thought verily that the bears would have ran unto him to devour him ; but God defended him, for the bears still made towards the ship after the men, that ran thither to save themselves. Meantime we and the man that fell into the cleft of ice took our advantage, and got into the ship on the other side; which the bears perceiving, they came fiercely towards us, that had no other arms to defend us withal but only the two halberds, which we doubting would not be sufficient, we still gave them work to do by throwing billets of firewood and other things at them, and every time we threw, they ran after them, as a dog useth to do at a stone that is cast at him. Meantime we sent a man down under hatches to strike fire, and another to fetch pikes; but we could get no fire, and so we had no means to shoot. At the last, as the bears came fiercely upon us, we struck one of them with a halberd upon the snout, wherewith she gave back when she felt herself hurt, and went away, which the other two, that were not so great as she, perceiving, ran away; and we thanked God that we were so well delivered from them, and so drew our sled quietly to our house, and there showed our men what had happened unto us.

The 26 of October the wind was north and north-north-west, with indifferent fair weather. Then we saw open water hard by the land, but we perceived the ice to drive in the sea still towards the ship.

The 27 of October the wind blew north-east, and it snowed so fast that we could not work without the door. That day our men killed a white fox, which they flayed, and after they had roasted it, ate thereof, which tasted like coney's flesh. The same day we set up our dial and made the clock strike, and we hung up a lamp to burn in the night time, wherein we used the fat of the bear, which we melted and burnt in the lamp.

The 3 of November the wind blew north-west with calm weather, and the sun rose south and by east and somewhat more southerly, and went down south and by west and somewhat more southerly; and then we could see nothing but the upper part of the sun above the horizon, and yet the land, where we were, was as high as the mast of our ship.

The 4 of November it was calm weather, but then we saw the sun no more, for it was no longer above the horizon. Then our chirurgeon made a bath, to bathe us in, of a wine pipe, wherein we entered one after the other, and it did us much good and was a great means of our health. The same day we took a white fox, that oftentimes came abroad, not as they used at other times; for that when the bears left us at the setting of the sun, and came not again before it rose, the foxes, to the contrary, came abroad when they were gone.

The 5 of November the wind was north and somewhat west, and then we saw open water upon the sea, but our ship lay still fast in the ice; and when the sun had left us, we saw the moon continually both day and night, and it never went down, when it was in the highest degree.

The 11 of November it was indifferent weather, the wind north-west. The same day we made a round hoop of cable yarn and like to a net, to catch foxes withal, that we might get them into the house, and it was made like a trap, which fell upon the foxes as they came under it; and that day we caught one.

The 12 of November the wind blew east, with a cloudy sky. That day we began to share our wine;

every man had two glasses a day, but commonly our
drink was water, which we melted out of snow, which
we gathered without the house.

The 13 of November it was foul weather, with
great snow, the wind east.

The 20 of November it was fair still weather, the
wind easterly.   Then we washed our shirts, but it
was so cold that, when we had washed and wrung them,
they presently froze so stiff that, although we laid
them by a great fire, the side that lay next the fire
thawed, but the other side was hard frozen; so that
we should sooner have torn them in sunder than
have opened them, whereby we were forced to put
them into the seething water again to thaw them. it
was so exceeding cold.

The 21 of November it was indifferent weather
with a north-east wind.   Then we agreed that every
man should take his turn to cleave wood, thereby to
ease our cook, that had more than work enough to do
twice a day, to dress meat and to melt snow for our
drink; but our master and the pilot were exempted
from that work.

The 22 of November the wind was south-east,
and it was fair weather; then we had but seventeen
cheeses, whereof one we ate amongst us, and the rest
were divided to every man one for his portion, which
they might eat when he list.

The 23 of November it was indifferent good
weather, the wind south-east, and as we perceived that
the foxes used to come oftener and more than they
were wont, to take them the better we made certain
traps of thick planks, whereon we laid stones, and
round about them placed ends of spars fast in the

ground, that they might not dig under them; and so got some of the foxes.

The 28 of November it was foul stormy weather, and the wind blew hard out of the north, and it snowed hard, whereby we were shut up again in our house, the snow lay so closed before the doors.

The 29 of November it was fair clear weather and a good air, the wind northerly; and we found means to open our door by shovelling away the snow, whereby we got one of our doors open; and going out we found all our traps and springes clean covered over with snow, which we made clean, and set them up again to take foxes; and that day we took one, which as then served us not only for meat, but of the skins we made caps to wear upon our heads, therewith to keep them warm from the extreme cold.

The 3 of December we had the like weather, at which times, as we lay in our cabins, we might hear the ice crack in the sea, and yet it was at the least two miles from us, which made a huge noise, and we were of opinion that as then the great hills of ice, which we had seen in the sea in summer time, brake one from the other. And for that during those two or three days, because of the extreme smoke, we made not so much fire as we commonly used to do, it froze so sore within the house, that the walls and the roof thereof were frozen two fingers thick with ice, and also in our cabins where we lay. All those three days, while we could not go out by reason of the foul weather, we set up the glass of twelve hours, and when it was run out, we set it up again, still watching it lest we should miss our time. For the cold was so great that our clock was frozen, and might not go, although we hung more weight on it than before.

The 6 of December it was foul weather again, with an easterly wind and extreme cold, almost not to be endured; whereupon we looked pitifully one upon the other, being in great fear that, if the extremity of the cold grew to be more and more, we should all die there with cold, for that what fire soever we made, it would not warm us: yea, and our sack, which is so strong, was frozen very hard, so that when we were every man to have his part, we were forced to melt it over the fire, which we shared every second day about half a pint for a man, wherewith we were forced to sustain ourselves; and at other times we drank water, which agreed not well with the cold, and we needed not to cool it with snow or ice, but we were forced to melt it out of the snow.

The 7 of December it was still foul weather, and we had a great storm with a north-east wind, which brought an extreme cold with it; at which time we knew not what to do, and while we sat consulting together what were best for us to do, one of our companions gave us counsel to burn some of the sea-coals that we had brought out of the ship, which would cast a great heat and continue long; and so at evening we made a great fire thereof, which cast a great heat. At which time we were very careful to keep it in, for that the heat being so great a comfort unto us, we took care how to make it continue long; whereupon we agreed to stop up all the doors and the chimney, thereby to keep in the heat, and so went into our cabins to sleep, well comforted with the heat, and so lay a great while talking together. But at last we were taken with a great swounding and dizziness in our heads, yet some more than other some, which we first perceived by a sick man and therefore the less able to bear it, and found ourselves to be very ill at ease, so that some of us that were strongest started out of their cabins, and first opened the chimney and then the doors, but he that opened the door fell down in a swound upon the snow.   Which I hearing, as lying in my cabin next to the door, started up, and casting vinegar in his face recovered him again, and so he rose up.   And when the doors were open, we all recovered our healths again by reason of the cold air; and so the cold, which before had been so great an enemy unto us, was then the only relief that we had, otherwise without doubt we had died in a sudden swound.   After that, the master, when we were come to ourselves again, gave every one of us a little wine to comfort our hearts.

The 8 of December it was foul weather, the wind northerly, very sharp and cold, but we durst lay no more coals on, as we did the day before, for that our misfortune had taught us that, to shun one danger, we should not run into another.

The 9 of December it was fair clear weather, the sky full of stars; then we set our door wide open, which before was fast closed up with snow, and made our springes ready to take foxes.

The 10 of December it was still fair starlight weather, the wind north-west.   Then we took two foxes, which were good meat for us, for as then our victuals began to be scant and the cold still increased, whereunto their skins served us for a good defence.

The 19 of December it was fair weather, the wind being south.   Then we put each other in good comfort that the sun was then almost half over, and ready to come to us again, which we sore longed for, it being a weary time for us to be without the sun, and to want the greatest comfort that God sendeth unto man here upon the earth, and that which rejoiceth every living thing.

The 20 of December before noon it was fair clear weather, and then we had taken a fox; but towards evening there rose such a storm in the south-west, with so great a snow, that all the house was enclosed therewith.

The 21 of December it was fair clear weather, with a north-east wind. Then we made our door clean again and made a way to go out, and cleansed our traps for the foxes, which did us great pleasure when we took them, for they seemed as dainty as venison unto us.

The 26 of December it was foul weather, the wind north-west, and it was so cold that we could not warm us, although we used all the means we could, with great fires, good store of clothes, and with hot stones and balls laid upon our feet and upon our bodies, as we lay in our cabins; but notwithstanding all this, in the morning our cabins were frozen white, which made us behold one the other with sad countenance. But yet we comforted ourselves again as well as we could, that the sun was then as low as it could go, and that it now began to come to us again, and we found it to be true; for that the days beginning to lengthen, the cold began to strengthen, but hope put us in good comfort and eased our pain.

The 27 of December it was still foul weather with a north-west wind, so that as then we had not been out in three days together, nor durst not thrust our heads out of doors; and within the house it was so extreme cold, that as we sat before a great fire, and seemed to burn on the fore side, we froze behind at our backs, and were all white, as the countrymen use to be, when they come in at the gates of the town in Holland with their sleds, and have gone all night.

The 28 of December it was still foul weather, with a west wind, but about evening it began to clear up. At which time one of our men made a hole open at one of our doors, and went out to see what news abroad, but found it so hard weather that he stayed not long, and told us that it had snowed so much, that the snow lay higher than our house, and that, if he had stayed out longer, his ears would undoubtedly have been frozen off.

The 29 of December it was calm weather and a cloudy sky, the wind being southward. That day he, whose turn it was, opened the door and digged a hole through the snow, where we went out of the house upon steps, as if it had been out of a cellar, at least seven or eight steps high, each step a foot from the other.

Anno 1597

After that, with great cold, danger, and disease, we had brought the year unto an end, we entered into the year of our Lord God 1597, the beginning whereof was in the same manner as the end of anno 1596 had been; for the weather continued as cold, foul, and snowy as it was before, so that upon the first of January we were enclosed in the house, the wind then being west. At the same time we agreed to share our wine, every man a small measure full, and that but once in two days. And as we were in great care and fear that it would be long before we should get out from thence, and we having but small hope therein, some of us spared to drink wine as long as we could, that, if we should stay long there, we might drink it at our need.

The 5 of January, when we had toiled all day, we remembered ourselves that it was Twelfth Even, and then we prayed our master that we might be merry that night, and said that we were content to spend some of the wine that night, which we had spared and which was our share every second day, and whereof for certain days we had not drunk; and so that night we made merry and drew for king. And therewith we had two pound of meal, whereof we made pancakes with oil, and we laid to every man a white biscuit, which we sopped in wine. And so, supposing that we were in our own country and amongst our friends, it comforted us as well as if we had made a great banquet in our own house. And we also distributed tickets, and our gunner was king of Nova Zembla, which is at least eight hundred miles long and lieth between two seas.

The 16 of January it was fair weather, the wind northerly; and then we went now and then out of the house to stretch out our joints and our limbs with going and running, that we might not become lame; and about noon time we saw a certain redness in the sky, as a show or messenger of the sun, that began to come towards us.

The 23 of January it was fair calm weather, with a south-west wind. Then four of us went to the ship and comforted each other, giving God thanks that the hardest time of the winter was past, being in good hope that we should live to talk of those things at home in our own country; and when we were in the ship, we found that the water rose higher and higher in it, and so each of us taking a biscuit or two with us, we went home again.

The 24 of January it was fair clear weather, with a west wind. Then I and Jacob Heemskerck, and another with us, went to the sea-side on the south side of Nova Zembla, where, contrary to our expectation, I, the first of all, saw the edge of the sun; wherewith we went speedily home again, to tell William Barents and the rest of our companions that joyful news. But William Barents, being a wise and well experienced pilot, would not believe it, esteeming it to be about fourteen days too soon for the sun to shine in that part of the world; but we earnestly affirmed the contrary and said we had seen the sun. Whereupon divers wagers were laid.

The 25 and 26 of January it was misty and close weather, so that we could not see anything. Then they, that laid the contrary wager with us, thought that they had won; but upon the twenty-seven day it was clear weather, and then we saw the sun in his full roundness above the horizon, whereby it manifestly appeared that we had seen it upon the twenty-four day of January.

The 26 of January in the evening the sick man, that was amongst us, was very weak, and felt himself to be extreme sick, for he had lain long time, and we comforted him as well as we might, and gave him the best admonition that we could, but he died not long after midnight.

The 27 of January it was fair clear weather, with a south-west wind. Then in the morning we digged a hole in the snow, hard by the house, but it was still so extreme cold that we could not stay long at work, and so we digged by turns, every man a little while, and then went to the fire, and another went and supplied his place, till at last we digged seven foot depth, where we went to bury the dead man. After that, when we had read certain chapters and sung some psalms, we all went out and buried the man; which done, we went in and broke our fasts. And while we were at meat, and discoursed amongst ourselves touching the great quantity of snow, that continually fell in that place, we said that, if it fell out that our house should be closed up again with snow, we would find the means to climb out at the chimney. Whereupon our master went to try if he could climb up through the chimney and so get out, and while he was climbing, one of our men went forth of the door to see if the master were out or not, who, standing upon the snow, saw the sun, and called us all out; wherewith we all went forth and saw the sun in his full roundness a little above the horizon. And then it was without all doubt that we had seen the sun upon the 24 of January, which made us all glad, and we gave God hearty thanks for his grace shewed unto us, that that glorious light appeared unto us again.

The 5 of February it was still foul weather, the wind being east with great store of snow, whereby we were shut up again into the house and had no other way to get out but by the chimney, and those, that could not climb out, were fain to help themselves within as well as they could.

The 12 of February it was clear weather and very calm, the wind south-west. Then we made our traps and springes clean again. Meantime there came a great bear towards our house, which made us all go in, and we levelled at her with our muskets, and as she came right before our door, we shot her into the breast clean through the heart, the bullet passing through her body and went out again at her tail, and was as flat as a counter. The bear feeling the blow, leapt backwards, and ran twenty or thirty foot from the house, and there lay down, wherewith we leapt all out of the house and ran to her, and found her still alive. And when she saw us, she reared up her head, as if she would gladly have done us some mischief; but we trusted her not, for that we had tried her strength sufficiently before, and therefore we shot her twice into the body again, and therewith she died. Then we ripped up her belly, and taking out her guts, drew her home to the house, where we flayed her and took at least one hundred pound of fat out of her belly, which we melted and burnt in our lamp. This grease did us great good service, for by that means we still kept a lamp burning all night long, which before we could not do for want of grease; and every man had means to burn a lamp in his cabin for such necessaries as he had to do. The bear's skin was nine foot long, and seven foot broad.

The 13 of February it was fair clear weather with a hard west wind, at which time we had more light in our house by burning of lamps, whereby we had means to pass the time away by reading and other exercises, which before (when we could not distinguish day from night by reason of the darkness, and had not lamps continually burning) we could not do.

The 18 of February it was foul weather with much snow and very cold, the wind being south-west; and in the night time, as we burnt lamps and some of our men lay awake, we heard beasts run upon the roof of our house, which by reason of the snow made the noise of their feet sound more than otherwise it would

How we shot a bear, wherefrom we got a good hundred pounds' weight of grease

have done, the snow was so hard and cracked so much that it gave a great sound, whereby we thought they had been bears; but when it was day, we saw no footing but of foxes, and we thought they had been bears, for the night, which of itself is solitary and fearful, made that which was doubtful to be more doubtful and worse feared.

The 22 of February it was clear fair weather with a south-west wind. Then we made ready a sled to fetch more wood, for need compelled us thereunto; for, as they say, hunger driveth the wolf out of the wood. And eleven of us went together, all well appointed with our arms; but coming to the place where we should have the wood, we could not come by it, by reason it lay so deep under the snow, whereby of necessity we were compelled to go further, where with great labour and trouble we got some; but as we returned back again therewith, it was so sore labour unto us that we were almost out of comfort, for that by reason of the long cold and trouble that we had endured, we were become so weak and feeble that we had little strength, and we began to be in doubt that we should lose our strength, and should not be able to fetch any more wood, and so we should have died with cold; but the present necessity, and the hope we had of better weather, increased our forces, and made us do more than our strengths afforded. And when we came near to our house, we saw much open water in the sea, which in long time we had not seen, which also put us in good comfort that things would be better.

The 3 of March it was fair weather, with a south-west wind; at which time our sick men were somewhat better, and sat upright in their cabins to do something to pass the time away, but after they found that they were too ready to stir before their times.

The 4 of March it was fair weather with a west wind. The same day there came a bear to our house, whom we watched with our pieces as we did before, and shot at her and hit her, but she run away. At that time five of us went to our ship, where we found that the bears had made work, and had opened our cook's cupboard, that was covered over with snow, thinking to find something in it, and had drawn it out of the ship, where we found it.

The 11 of March twelve of us went to the place where we used to go, to fetch a sled of wood, but still we had more pain and labour therewith, because we were weaker; and when we came home with it and were very weary, we prayed the master to give either of us a draught of wine, which he did, wherewith we were somewhat relieved and comforted, and after that were the willinger to labour, which was unsupportable for us, if mere extremity had not compelled us thereunto, saying oftentimes one unto the other, that if the wood were to be bought for money, we would give all our earnings or wages for it.

The 3 of April it was fair clear weather, with a north-east wind and very calm; then we made a staff to play at golf, thereby to stretch our joints, which we sought, by all the means we could, to do.

The 6 of April it was still foul weather, with a stiff north-west wind. That night there came a bear to our house, and we did the best we could to shoot at her, but because it was moist weather and the powder damp, our piece would not give fire, wherewith the bear came boldly toward the house, and came down the stairs close to the door, seeking to break into the house; but our master held the door fast to, and being in great haste and fear, could not bar it with the piece of wood that we used thereunto; but the bear seeing that the door was shut, she went back again, and within two hours after she came again, and went round about and upon the top of the house, and made such a roaring, that it was fearful to hear, and at last got to the chimney, and made such work there, that we thought she would have broken it down, and tore the sail, that was made fast about it, in many pieces with a great and fearful noise; but for that it was night we made no resistance against her, because we could not see her.   At last she went away and left us.

The 15 of April it was fair calm weather with a north wind; then seven of us went aboard the ship to see in what case it was, and found it to be all in one sort; and as we came back again there came a great bear towards us, against whom we began to make defence; but she perceiving that, made away from us, and we went to the place from whence she came, to see her den, where we found a great hole made in the ice, about a man's length in depth, the entry thereof being very narrow, and within wide.   There we thrust in our pikes to feel if there was anything within it, but perceiving it was empty, one of our men crept into it, but not too far, for it was fearful to behold.   After that we went along by the sea side, and there we saw that in the end of March and the beginning of April the ice was in such wonderful manner risen and piled up one upon the other, that it was wonderful, in such manner as if there had been whole towns made of ice, with towers and bulwarks round about them.

The 16 of April it was foul weather, the wind north-west, whereby the ice began somewhat to break.

The 17 of April it was fair clear weather with a south-west wind; and then seven of us went to the ship, and there we saw open water in the sea, and then we went over the ice hills as well as we could to the water, for in six or seven months we had not gone so near unto it; and when we got to the water, there we saw a little bird swimming therein, but as soon as it espied us, it dived under the water, which we took for a sign that there was more open water in the sea than there had been before, and that the time approached that the water would be open.

The 29 of April it was fair weather with a south-west wind. Then we played at golf, both to the ship and from thence again homeward, to exercise ourselves.

The 30 of April it was fair weather, the wind south-west; then in the night we could see the sun in the north, when it was in the highest, just above the horizon, so that from that time we saw the sun both night and day.

The 1 of May it was fair weather with a west wind; then we sod our last flesh, which for a long time we had spared, and it was still very good, and the last morsel tasted as well as the first, only it had but one fault, which was that it would last no longer.

The 2 of May it was foul weather with a storm out of the south-west, whereby the sea was almost clear of ice, and then we began to speak about getting from thence, for we had kept house long enough there.

The 3 of May it was still foul weather with a south-west wind, whereby the ice began wholly to drive away, but it lay fast about the ship. And when our best meat, as flesh, barley, and other things, began to fail us, which was our greatest sustenance, and that it behoved us to be somewhat strong, to sustain the labour that we were to undergo when we went from thence, the master shared the rest of the pork amongst us, which was a small barrel with salt pork in pickle, whereof every one of us had two ounces a day, which continued for the space of three weeks, and then it was eaten up.

The 4 of May it was indifferent fair weather, the wind south-west. That day five of us went to the ship, and found it lying still as fast in the ice, more than before; for about the middle of March it was but 75 paces from the open water, and now it was 500 paces from the water and enclosed round about with high hills of ice, which put us in no small fear how we should bring our scute and our boat through or over that way into the water, when we went to leave that place.

The 9 of May it was fair clear weather with an indifferent wind out of the north-east; at which time the desire, that our men had to be gone from thence, still more and more increased, and then they agreed to speak to William Barents to move the master to go from thence, but he held them off with fair words; and yet it was not done in a mutinous manner, but to take the best counsel with reason and good advice, for they let themselves easily be talked over.

The 20 of May at noon we spake unto the master, and told him that it was time to make preparation to be gone, if he would ever get away from thence; whereunto he made answer that his own life was as dear unto him as any of ours unto us, nevertheless he willed us to make haste to prepare our clothes and other things ready and fit for our voyage, and that in the meantime we should patch and amend them, that after it might be no hindrance unto us, and that we should stay till the month of May was past, and then make ready the scute and the boat and all other things fit and convenient for our journey.

The 22 of May it was fair weather with a north-west wind; and for that we had almost spent all our wood, we brake the portal of our door down and burnt it.

The 28 of May it was foul weather with a north-west wind; after noon it began to be somewhat better. Then seven of us went unto the ship, and fetched such things from thence as should serve us for the furnishing of our scute and our boat, as the old foresail to make the sails for our boat and our scute, and some tackles and other things necessary for us.

The 29 of May, in the morning, it was reasonable fair weather with a west wind. Then ten of us went unto the scute to bring it to the house to dress it and make it ready to sail, but we found it deep hidden under the snow, and were fain with great pain and labour to dig it out; but when we had gotten it out of the snow, and thought to draw it to the house, we could not do it, because we were too weak. Wherewith we became wholly out of heart, doubting that we should not be able to go forward with our labour; but the master encouraging us bade us strive to do more than we were able, saying that both our lives and our welfare consisted therein, and that if we could not get the scute from thence and make it ready, then he said we must dwell there as burghers of Nova Zembla, and make our graves in that place. But there wanted no good will in us, but only strength, which made us for that time to leave off work and let the scute lie still, which was no small grief unto us and trouble to think what were best for us to do. But after noon, being thus comfortless come home, we took heart again, and determined to turn the boat, that lay by the house with her keel upwards, and to amend it and heighten the gunwales, that it might be the fitter to carry us over the sea; for we made full account that we had a long, trouble-some voyage in hand, wherein we might have many crosses, and wherein we should not be sufficiently provided for all things necessary, although we took

How we made ready to sail back again to Holland

never so much care. And while we were busy about our work there came a great bear unto us. Where-with we went into our house and stood to watch her in our three doors with arquebuses, and one stood in the chimney with a musket. This bear came boldlier unto us than ever any had done before; for she came to the nether step that went to one of our doors, and the man that stood in the door saw her not, because he looked towards the other door. But they that stood within saw her and in great fear called to him, wherewith he turned about, and although he was in a maze he shot at her, and the bullet passed clean through her body: whereupon she ran away. Yet it was a fearful thing to see, for the bear was almost upon him before he saw her, so that if the piece had failed to give fire (as oftentimes they do) it had cost him his life, and it may be that the bear would have gotten into the house. The bear being gone somewhat from the house, lay down. Wherewith we went all armed and killed her outright, and when we had ripped open her belly we found a piece of a buck therein, with hair, skin and all, which not long before she had torn and devoured.

The 30 of May it was indifferent fair weather, not very cold, but dark, the wind west. Then we began to set ourselves to work about the boat to amend it, the rest staying in the house to make the sails and all other things ready that were necessary for us. But while we were busy working at our boat, there came a bear unto us, wherewith we were forced to leave work; but she was shot by our men. Then we brake down the planks of the roof of our house, to amend our boat withal, and so proceeded in our work as well as we could; for every man was willing to labour, for we had sore longed for it, and did more than we were able to do.

The 31 of May it was fair weather, but somewhat colder than before, the wind being south-west, whereby the ice drave away, and we wrought hard about our boat. But when we were in the chiefest part of work, there came another bear, as if they had smelt that we

would be gone, and that therefore they desired to taste
a piece of some of us; for that was the third day, one
after the other, that they set so fiercely upon us. So that
we were forced to leave our work and go into the house,
and she followed us; but we stood with our pieces to
watch her, and shot three pieces at her, two from our
doors and one out of the chimney, which all three hit
her, whereby she fared as the dog did with the pudding.
But her death did us more hurt than her life, for after
we ripped her belly, we dressed her liver and ate it,
which in the taste liked us well, but it made us all sick,
specially three that were exceeding sick, and we verily
thought that we should have lost them, for all their
skins came off from the foot to the head. But yet they
recovered again, for the which we gave God hearty
thanks; for if as then we had lost these three men, it
was a hundred to one that we should never have gotten
from thence, because we should have had too few men
to draw and lift at our need.

The 3 of June, in the morning, it was fair clear
weather, the wind west; and then we were somewhat
better, and took great pains with the boat, that at
last we got it ready, after we had wrought six days upon
it.   About evening it began to blow hard, and therewith the water was very open, which put us in good
comfort that our deliverance would soon follow, and
that we should once get out of that desolate and
fearful place.

The 4 of June it was fair clear weather and indifferent
warm; and about the south-east sun (half past 7 a.m.)
eleven of us went to our scute where it then lay, and
drew it towards the ship.   At which time the labour
seemed lighter unto us than it did before, when we took

it in hand and were forced to leave it off again. The reason thereof was the opinion that we had, that the snow as then lay harder upon the ground, and so was become stronger, and it may be that our courages were better to see that the time gave us open water, and that our hope was that we should get from thence. And so three of our men stayed by the scute to build her to our minds; and for that it was a herring scute, which are made narrow behind, therefore they sawed it off behind, and made it a broad stern and better to brook the seas. They built it also somewhat higher, and dressed it up as well they could. The rest of our men were busy in the house to make all other things ready for our voyage, and that day drew two sleds with victuals and other goods unto the ship, that lay about half way between the house and the open water, so that after they might have so much the shorter way to carry the goods unto the water side, when we should go away. At which time all the labour and pains that we took seemed light and easy unto us, because of the hope that we had to get out of that wild, desert, irksome, fearful, and cold country.

The 11 of June it was foul weather and it blew hard north-north-west, so that all day we could do nothing, and we were in great fear lest the storm would carry the ice and the ship both away together (which might well have come to pass); then we should have been in greater misery than ever we were, for that our goods, both victuals and others, were then all in the ship; but God provided so well for us, that it fell not out so unfortunately.

The 12 of June it was indifferent fair weather. Then we went with hatchets, halberds, shovels, and other instruments, to make the way plain where we should draw the scute and the boat to the water side, along the way that lay full of knobs and hills of ice, where we wrought sore with our hatchets and other instruments. And while we were in the chiefest of our work, there came a great lean bear out of the sea upon the ice towards us, which we judged to come out of Tartaria, for we had seen of them 80 or 120 miles within the sea. And for that we had no muskets, but only one which our surgeon carried, I ran in great haste towards the ship to fetch one or two, which the bear perceiving ran after me, and was very likely to have overtaken me; but our company seeing that, left their work and ran after her, which made the bear turn towards them and left me. But when she ran towards them, she was shot into the body by the surgeon, and ran away; but because the ice was so uneven and hilly, she could not go far, but being by us overtaken, we killed her outright, and smote her teeth out of her head, while she was yet living.

The 13 of June it was fair weather. Then the master and the carpenters went to the ship, and there made the scute and the boat ready, so that there rested nothing as then, but only to bring it down to the water side. The master and those that were with him, seeing that it was open water and a good west wind, came back to the house again, and there he spake unto William Barents (that had been long sick), and showed him that he thought it good (seeing it was a fit time) to go from thence, and so willed the company to drive the boat and the scute down to the water side, and in the name of God to begin our voyage to sail from Nova Zembla. Then William Barents wrote a letter, which

How we prepared a way whereby we brought our boats and goods to the sea

he put into a musket's charge and hanged it up in the chimney, showing how we came out of Holland to sail to the kingdom of China, and what had happened unto us being there on land, with all our crosses, that if any man chanced to come thither, they might know what had happened unto us, and how we had been forced in our extremity to make that house, and had dwelt 10 months therein. And for that we were now forced to put to sea in two small open boats and to undertake a dangerous and adventurous voyage in hand, the master wrote two letters, which most of us subscribed unto, signifying how we had stayed there upon the land in great trouble and misery, in hope that our ship would be freed from the ice and that we should sail away with it again, and how it fell out to the contrary, and that the ship lay fast in the ice; so that in the end, the time passing away and our victuals beginning to fail us, we were forced, for the saving of our own lives, to leave the ship and to sail away in our open boats, and so to commit ourselves into the hands of God. Of which letters each boat had one, that if we chanced to lose one another, or that by storms or any other misadventure we happened to be cast away, that then by the scute that escaped men might know how we left each other. And so, having finished all things as we determined, we drew the boat to the water side and left a man in it, and went and fetched the scute, and after that eleven sleds with goods, as victuals and some wine that yet remained, and the merchants' goods, of which we took every care to preserve as much as was possible, viz., six packs with fine woollen cloth, a chest with linen, two packets with velvet, two small chests with money, two dryfats with the men's clothes and other things,

13 barrels of bread, a barrel of cheese, a flitch of bacon, two runlets of oil, six small runlets of wine, two runlets of vinegar, with other packs belonging to the sailors; so that when they lay all together upon a heap, a man would have judged that they would not have gone into the scutes. Which being all put into them, we went to the house, and first drew William Barents upon a sled to the place where our scutes lay, and after that we fetched Nicholas Andrewson, both of them having been long sick. And so we entered into the scutes and divided ourselves into each of them alike, and put into either of them a sick man. Then the master caused both the scutes to lie close one by the other, and there we subscribed to the letters which he had written. And so committing ourselves to the will and mercy of God, with a west-north-west wind and an indifferent open water, we set sail and put to sea.

The 14 of June, in the morning, the sun easterly, we put off from the land of Nova Zembla and the fast ice thereunto adjoining, with our boat and our scute, having a west wind, and sailed east-north-east all that day to Island Point, which was 20 miles; but our first beginning was not very good, for we entered fast into the ice again, which there lay very hard and fast; which put us into no small fear and trouble. And being there, four of us went on land, to know the situation thereof, and there we took four birds, which we killed with stones upon the cliffs.

The 15 of June the ice began to go away; then we put to sail again with a south wind, and passed along by the Head Point and Flushing Point, stretching most north-east, and after that north, to Cape Desire, which is about 52 miles, and there we lay till the 16 of June.

The 16 of June we set sail again, and got to the Islands of Orange with a south wind, which is 32 miles distant from Cape Desire. There we went on land with two small barrels and a kettle, to melt snow and to put the water into the barrels, as also to seek for birds and eggs to make meat for our sick men. And being there, we made fire with such wood as we found there, and melted the snow, but found no birds; but three of our men went over the ice to the other island, and got three birds, and as we came back again our master (which was one of the three) fell into the ice, where he was in great danger of his life, for in that place there ran a great stream; but by God's help he got out again and came to us, and there dried himself by the fire that we had made; at which fire we drest the birds, and carried them to the scute to our sick men, and filled our two runlets with water, that held about eight quarts apiece. Which done, we put to the sea again with a south-east wind and drowsy mizzling weather, whereby we were all dankish and wet, for we had no shelter in our open scutes, and sailed west and west and by south to the Ice Point. And being there, both our scutes lying hard by each other, the master called to William Barents to know how he did, and William Barents made answer and said, "Well, God be thanked, and I hope, before we get to Warehouse, to be able to go." Then he spake to me and said, "Gerrit, are we about the Ice Point? If we be, then I pray you lift me up, for I must view it once again." At which time we had sailed from the Islands of Orange to the Ice Point, about 20 miles; and then the wind went round to the west, and we made our scutes fast to a great piece of ice, and there ate somewhat. But the weather was still fouler and fouler, so that we were once again enclosed with ice and forced to stay there.

The 17 of June, in the morning, when we had broken our fasts, the ice came so fast upon us, that it made our hairs stand upright upon our heads, it was so fearful to behold. By which means we could not save our scutes, so that we thought verily that it was a foreshowing of our last end; for we drave away so hard with the ice, and were so sore pressed between a flake of ice, that we thought verily the scutes would burst in a hundred pieces, which made us look pitifully one upon the other, for no counsel nor advice was to be found, but every minute of an hour we saw death before our eyes. At last, being in this discomfort and extreme necessity, the master said, if we could take hold with a rope upon the fast ice, we might therewith draw the scute up, and so get it out of the great drift of ice. But as this counsel was good, yet it was so full of danger, that it was the hazard of his life, that should take upon him to do it; and without doing it, was it most certain that it would cost us all our lives. This counsel (as I said) was good, but no man (like to the tale of the mice) durst hang the bell about the cat's neck, fearing to be drowned; yet necessity required to have it done, and the most danger made us choose the least. So that being in that perplexity, I being the lightest of all our company, took on me to fasten a rope upon the fast ice; and so creeping from one piece of driving ice to another, by God's help got to the fast ice, where I made a rope fast to a high howell, and they that were in the scute drew it thereby unto the said fast ice, and then one man alone could draw more than all of them could have done before. And

when we had gotten thither, in all haste we took our
sick men out and laid them upon the ice, laying clothes
and other things under them, and then took all our
goods out of the scutes, and so drew them upon the
ice, whereby for that time we were delivered from that
great danger, making account that we had escaped
out of death's claws, as it was most true.

The 18 of June we repaired and amended our
scutes again, being much bruised and crushed with the
racking of the ice, and were forced to drive all the nails
fast again, and to piece many things about them,
God sending us wood wherewith we molt our pitch,
and did all other things that belonged thereunto.
That done, some of us went upon the land to seek for
eggs, which the sick men longed for, but we could find
none; but we found four birds, not without great
danger of our lives between the ice and the firm land,
wherein we often fell, and were in no small danger.

The 19 of June it was indifferent weather, the
wind north-west and west-south-west, but we were still
shut up in the ice and saw no opening, which made us
think that there would be our last abode, and that we
should never get from thence; but on the other side
we comforted ourselves again, that seeing God had
helped us oftentimes unexpectedly in many perils, and
that His arm as yet was not shortened, but that He
could help us at His goodwill and pleasure, it made us
somewhat comfortable, and caused us to speak cheer-
fully one unto the other.

The 20 of June it was indifferent weather, the
wind west, and when the sun was south-east, Nicholas
Andrewson began to be extreme sick, whereby we
perceived that he would not live long, and the boatswain

came into our scute and told us in what case he was, and that he could not long continue alive. Whereupon William Barents spake and said, "I think I shall not live long after him"; and yet we did not judge William Barents to be so sick, for we sat talking one with the other, and spake of many things, and William Barents looked at my card which I had made touching our voyage. At last he laid away the card and spake unto me, saying, "Gerrit, give me some drink;" and he had no sooner drunk, but he was taken with so sudden a qualm, that he turned his eyes in his head, and died presently, and we had no time to call the master out of the other scute to speak unto him; and so he died before Nicholas Andrewson. The death of William Barents put us in no small discomfort, as being the chief guide and only pilot on whom we reposed ourselves next under God; but we could not strive against God, and therefore we must of force be content.

The 21 of June the ice began to drive away again, and God made us some opening with a south-south-west wind; and when the sun was north-west, the wind began to blow south-east with a good gale, and we began to make preparations to go from thence.

The 22 of June, in the morning, it blew a good gale out of the south-east, and then the sea was reasonable open; but we were forced to draw our scutes over the ice to get unto it, which was great pain and labour unto us. For first we were forced to draw our scutes over a piece of ice of 50 paces long, and there put them into the water, and then again to draw them up upon other ice, and after draw them at the least 300 paces more over the ice, before we could bring them to a good place, where we might easily get out. And being gotten unto the open water, we committed ourselves to God and set sail, the sun being about east-north-east, with an indifferent gale of wind out of the south and south-south-east, and sailed west and west and by south, till the sun was south; and then we were round about enclosed with ice again, and could not get out, but were forced to lie still.   But not long after, the ice opened again like to a sluice, and we passed through it and set sail again, and so sailed along by the land, but were presently enclosed with ice; but being in hope of opening again, meantime we ate somewhat, for the ice went not away as it did before. After that, we used all the means we could to break it, but all in vain; and yet, a good while after, the ice opened again, and we got out and sailed along by the land, west and by south, with a south wind.

The 23 of June we sailed still forward west and by south till the sun was south-east, and got to Cape Comfort.

The 25 of June it blew a great south wind, and the ice whereunto we made ourselves fast was not very strong, whereby we were in great fear, that we should break off from it and drive into the sea; for when the sun was in the west, a piece of that ice brake off, whereby we were forced to dislodge and make ourselves fast to another piece of ice.

The 26 of June it still blew hard out of the south, and broke the ice, whereunto we were fast, in pieces; and we thereby drave into the sea, and could get no more to the fast ice, whereby we were in a thousand dangers to be all cast away.   And driving in that sort in the sea, we rowed as much as we could, but we could not get near unto the land: therefore we hoised up our foresail, and tried to do it with our sails. But our foremast brake twice in pieces, and then it was worse for us than before; and notwithstanding that there blew a great gale of wind, yet we were forced to hoise up our main-sail. But the wind blew so hard into it, that, if we had not presently taken it in again, we had been capsized, or else our boat would have been filled with water. For the water began to leap over board, and we were a good way in the sea, at which time the waves went so hollow that it was most fearful, and we thereby saw nothing but death before our eyes, and every twinkling of an eye looked when we should sink. But God, that had delivered us out of so many dangers of death, holp us once again, and contrary to our expectations sent us a north-west wind, and so with great danger we got to the fast ice again. When we were delivered out of that danger, and knew not where our other scute was, we sailed four miles along by the fast ice, but found it not. Whereby we were wholly out of heart and in great fear that they were drowned; at which time it was misty weather. And so sailing along, and hearing no news of our other scute, we shot off a musket, which they hearing shot off another, but yet we could not see each other. Meantime, approaching nearer to each other, and the weather waxing somewhat clearer, as we and they shot once again, we saw the smoke of their pieces; and at last we met together again, and saw them lie fast between driving and fast ice. And when we got near unto them, we went over the ice and holp them to unlade the goods out of their scute, and drew it over the ice, and with much pain and trouble brought it into the open water again; and while they were fast in the ice, they had found some wood upon the land by the sea side; and when we lay by each other, we sod some bread and water together and ate it up warm, which did us much good.

The 28 of June, when the sun was in the east, we laid all our goods upon the ice, and then drew the scutes upon the ice also, because we were so hardly pressed on all sides with the ice, and the wind came out of the sea upon the land, and therefore we were in fear to be wholly enclosed with the ice, and should not be able to get out thereof again. And being upon the ice, we made a tent of our sails, and lay down to rest, appointing one of our men to keep watch. And when the sun was north there came three bears towards our scutes, wherewith he that kept the watch cried, "Three bears! three bears!" At which noise we leapt out of our boats with our muskets, that were laden with hail-shot to shoot at birds, and had no time to discharge them, and therefore shot at them therewith. And although that kind of shot could not hurt them much, yet they ran away; and in the meantime they gave us leisure to load our muskets with bullets, and by that means we shot one of the three dead. Which the other two perceiving, ran away, but within two hours after they came again; but when they were almost at us and heard us make a noise, they ran away. At which time the wind was west and west and by north, which made the ice drive with great force into the east.

The 29 of June, the sun being south-south-west, the two bears came again to the place where the dead bear lay, where one of them took the dead bear in his mouth, and went a great way with it over the rugged ice, and then began to eat it. Which we perceiving,

shot a musket at her, but she hearing the noise thereof,
ran away, and let the dead bear lie. Then four of us
went thither, and saw that in so short a time she had
eaten almost the half of her; and we took the dead
bear and laid it upon a high heap of ice, so that we
might see it out of our scute, that if the bear came
again we might shoot at her. At which time we found
out the great strength of the bear, that carried the
dead bear as lightly in her mouth, as if it had been
nothing; whereas we four had enough to do, to carry
away the half dead bear between us. Then the wind
still held west, which drave the ice into the east.

The 1 of July it was indifferent fair weather, with
a west-north-west wind; and in the morning, the sun
being east, there came a bear from the driving ice, and
swam over the water to the fast ice, whereon we lay;
but when she heard us, she came no nearer, but ran
away. And when the sun was south-east, the ice
came so fast in towards us, that all the ice, whereon
we lay with our scutes and our goods, brake and ran
one piece upon another; whereby we were in no small
difficulty, for at that time most of our goods fell into
the water. But we with great diligence drew our scute
further upon the ice towards the land, where we thought
to be better defended from the driving of the ice. And
as we went to fetch our goods, we fell into the greatest
trouble that ever we had before; for that we endured
so great danger in the saving thereof, that as we laid
hold upon one piece thereof, the rest sunk down with the
ice, and many times the ice brake under our own feet.
Whereby we were wholly discomforted and in a manner
clean out of all hope, expecting no issue thereof; in
such sort that our trouble at that time surmounted all

our former cares and impeachments. And when we
thought to draw up our boat upon the ice, the ice
brake under us, and we were carried away with the
scute and all by the driving ice; and when we thought
to save the goods, the ice brake under our feet, and
with that the scute brake in many places, especially
that which we had mended, as the mast, the mast
plank, and almost all the scute, wherein one of our
men that was sick and a chest of money lay, which
we with great danger of our lives got out from it.   For
as we were doing it, the ice that was under our feet
drave from us and slid away under the other ice;
whereby we were in danger to burst both our arms
and our legs.   At which time, thinking that we had
been clean quit of our scute, we beheld each other
in pitiful manner, knowing not what we should do,
our lives depending thereon.   But God made so good
provision for us, that the pieces of ice drave from each
other; wherewith we ran in great haste unto the scute
and drew it to us again in such case as it was, and
laid it upon the fast ice by the boat, where it was in
more security; which put us unto an exceeding and
great and dangerous labour, from the time that the
sun was south-east until it was west-south-west.   And
in all that time we rested not, which made us extreme
weary and wholly out of comfort; for that it troubled
us sore, and it was much more fearful unto us, than at
that time when William Barents died; for there we
were almost drowned, and that day we lost (which was
sunk in the sea) two barrels of bread, a chest with linen
cloth, a dryfat with the sailors' clothes, our astrono-
mical ring, a pack of scarlet cloth, a runlet of oil, and
some cheeses, and a runlet of wine, which bunged

with the ice, so that there was not anything thereof saved.

The 2 of July, the sun east, there came another bear unto us, but we making a noise, she ran away; and when the sun was west-south-west it began to be fair weather. Then we began to mend our scute with the planks wherewith we had made the bottom boards; and while six of us were busied about mending of our scute, the other six went further into the land, to seek for some wood, and to fetch some stones to lay upon the ice, that we might make a fire thereon, therewith to melt our pitch, which we should need about the scute, as also to see if they could fetch any wood for a mast; which they found with certain stones, and brought them where the scutes lay. And when they came to us again, they shewed us that they had found certain wood, which had been cloven, and brought some wedges with them, wherewith the said wood had been cloven; whereby it appeared that men had been there. Then we made all the haste we could to make a fire, and to melt our pitch, and to do all other things that were necessary to be done for the repairing of our scute, so that we got it ready again by that the sun was north-east; at which time also we roasted our birds and made a good meal with them.

The 3 of July, in the morning, the sun being east, two of our men went to the water, and there they found two of our oars, our helm stick, the pack of scarlet cloth, the chest with linen cloth, and a hat that fell out of the dryfat; whereby we guessed that it was broken in pieces. Which they perceiving, took as much with them as they could carry, and came unto us, showing us that they had left more goods behind them.

Whereupon the master with five more of us went thither, and drew all the goods upon the firm ice, that when we went away we might take it with us; but they could not carry the chest nor the pack of cloth (that were full of water), because of their weight; but were forced to let them stand till we went away, that the water might drop out of them, and we might afterwards fetch them, as we did. The sun being south-west, there came another great bear unto us, which the man that kept watch saw not, and had been devoured by her, if one of our other men from out of the boat had not espied her, and called to him that kept watch to look to himself, who therewith ran away. Meantime the bear was shot into the body, but she escaped; and that time the wind was east-north-east.

The 10 of July, from the time that the sun was east-north-east till it was east, we took great pains and labour to get through the ice; and at last we got through and rowed forth, until we happened to fall between two great fields of ice, that closed one with the other, so that we could not get through, but were forced to draw the scutes upon them, and to unlade the goods, and then to draw them over to the open water on the other side; and then we must go fetch the goods also to the same place, being at least 110 paces long, which was very hard for us; but there was no remedy, for it was but a folly for us to think of any weariness. And when we were in the open water again, we rowed forward as well as we could, but we had not rowed long before we fell between two great fields of ice, that came driving one against the other; but by God's help and our speedy rowing we got from between them, before they closed up; and being through, we had a hard west wind right in our teeth, so that of force we were constrained to make towards the fast ice that lay by the shore, and at last with much trouble we got unto it. And being there, we thought to row along by the fast ice unto an island that we saw before us; but by reason of the hard contrary wind we could not go far, so that we were compelled to draw the scutes and the goods upon the ice, to see what issue God would send us. But our courages were cooled to see ourselves so often enclosed in the ice, being in great fear that by means of the long and continual pains (which we were forced to take) we should lose all our strength, and by that means should not long be able to continue or hold out.

The 11 of July, in the morning, as we sat fast upon the ice, the sun being north-east, there came a great bear out of the water running towards us; but we watched for her with three muskets, and when she came within 30 paces of us, we shot all the three muskets at her and killed her outright, so that she stirred not a foot, and we might see the fat run out at the holes of her skin, that was shot in with the muskets, swim upon the water like oil. And so driving dead upon the water, we went upon a field of ice to her, and putting a rope about her neck, drew her up upon the ice and smit out her teeth; at which time we measured her body, and found it to be eight foot thick. Then we had a west wind with dirty weather; but when the sun was south, it began to clear up. Then three of our men went to the island that lay before us, and being there, they saw the Cross Island lying westward from them, and went thither, to see if that summer there had been any Russian there, and went thither upon the fast ice that lay between the two islands; and

being in the island, they could not perceive that any
man had been in it, since we were there.   There they
got 70 burrow-ducks' eggs, but when they had them,
they knew not wherein to carry them.   At last one of
them put off his breeches, and tying them fast below,
they carried them between two of them, and the third
bare the musket; and so they came to us again, after
they had been twelve hours out, which put us in no
small fear to think what was become of them.   They
told us that they had many times gone up to the knees
in water upon the ice between both the islands, and
it was at least 24 miles to and fro that they had gone;
which made us wonder how they could endure it, seeing
we were all so weak.   With the eggs that they had
brought, we were all well comforted, and fared like
lords, so that we found some relief in our great misery;
and then we shared our last wine amongst us, whereof
everyone had three glasses.

The 18 of July, about the east sun, three of our
men went up upon the highest part of the land, to see
if there was any open water in the sea.   At which time
they saw much open water, but it was so far from the
land, that they were almost out of comfort, because
it lay so far from the land and the fast ice, being of
opinion that we should not be able to draw the scutes
and the goods so far thither, because our strength
failed us more and more, and the sore labour and pain,
that we were forced to endure, more and more increased.
And coming to our scutes, they brought us that news;
but we, being compelled thereunto by necessity,
abandoned all weariness and faint-heartedness, and
determined with ourselves to bring the boats and the
goods to the water side, and to row unto that ice, where

we must pass over, to get to the open water.   And when
we got to it, we unladed our scutes, and drew them
first over the ice to the open water, and after that the
goods, it being at the least 1000 paces.   Which was so
sore a labour for us, that, as we were in hand therewith,
we were in a manner ready to leave off in the middle
thereof, and feared that we should not go through
withal.   But for that we had gone through so many
dangers, we hoped that we should not be faint therein,
wishing that it might be the last trouble, that we should
as then endure; and so with great difficulty got into
the open water about the south-west sun.   Then we
set sail till the sun was west and by south, and presently
fell amongst the ice again, where we were forced to
draw up the scutes again upon the ice; and being upon
it, we could see the Cross Island, which we guessed
to be about four miles from us, the wind then being
east and east-north-east.

The 19 of July, lying in that manner upon the
ice, about the east sun seven of our men went to the
Cross Island, and being there, they saw great store of
open water in the west; wherewith they much rejoiced,
and made as great haste as they could to get to the
scutes again; but before they came away, they got a
hundred eggs, and brought them away with them.
And coming to the scutes, they showed us that they
had seen as much open water in the sea as they could
discern; being in good hope that that would be the
last time, that they should draw the scutes over the
ice, and that it should be no more measured by us, and
in that sort put us in good comfort.   Whereupon we
made speed to dress our eggs, and shared them amongst
us; and presently, the sun being south-south-west,

we fell to work, to make all things ready to bring the
scutes to the water, which were to be drawn at least
270 paces over the ice; which we did with a good
courage, because we were in good hope, that it would
be the last time. And getting to the water, we put to
sea, with God's help, with an east and east-north-east
wind and a good gale, so that with the west sun we
passed by the Cross Island, which is distant from Cape
Nassau 40 miles. And presently, after that, the ice
left us, and we got clear out of it; yet we saw some
in the sea, but it troubled us not. And so we held our
course west and by south, with a good gale of wind
out of the east and east-north-east, so that we guessed
that between every meal-tide we sailed 72 miles;
wherewith we were exceedingly comforted, giving God
thanks, that He had delivered us out of so great and
many difficulties (wherein it seemed that we should
have been overwhelmed), hoping in His mercy, that
from thenceforth He would aid us.

The 20 of July, having still a good gale, about
the south-east sun we passed along by the Black
Point, which is 48 miles distant from the Cross Island,
and sailed west-south-west; and about the evening,
with the west sun, we saw the Admiralty Island, and
about the north sun passed along by it, which is distant
from the Black Point 32 miles. And passing along
by it, we saw about two hundred sea-horses lying upon
a field of ice, and we sailed close by them and drave
them from thence, which had almost cost us dear;
for they, being mighty strong and of great force,
swam towards us (as if they would be revenged on us
for the despite that we had done them) round about
our scutes with a great noise, as if they would have

devoured us; but we escaped from them by reason that we had a good gale of wind, yet it was not wisely done of us to wake sleeping wolves.

The 28 of July it was fair weather, with a north-east wind. Then we sailed along by the land, and with the south-west sun got before St Laurence Bay, or Sconce Point, and sailed south-east 24 miles; and

True portraiture of our boats, and how we nearly got into trouble with the sea-horses

being there, we found two Russians' lodgies or ships beyond the Point, wherewith we were not a little comforted to think that we were come to the place where we found men, but were in some doubt of them because they were so many, for at that time we saw at least 30 men, and knew not what sort of persons they were. There with much pain and labour we got

to the land, which they perceiving, left off their work
and came towards us, but without any arms; and
we also went on shore, as many as were well, for
divers of us were very ill at ease and weak by reason
of the scurvy.   And when we met together we saluted
each other in friendly wise, they after theirs, and we
after our manner.   And when we were met, both
they and we looked each other stedfastly in the face,
for that some of them knew us, and we them to be
the same men, which the year before, when we passed
through the Weygats, had been in our ship.   At which
time we perceived that they were abashed and wondered
at us, to remember that at that time we were so well
furnished with a great ship, that was exceedingly
provided of all things necessary, and then to see us so
lean and bare, and with so small scutes into that country.
And amongst them there were two, that in friendly
manner clapt the master and me upon the shoulder,
as knowing us since the former voyage; for there was
none of all our men that was as then in the Weygats,
but we two only; and they asked us for our crable,
meaning our ship, and we shewed them by signs, as well
as we could (for we had no interpreter), that we had lost
our ship in the ice.   Wherewith they said, "*Crable pro
pal*?" which we understood to be, "Have you lost your
ship?"   And we made answer, "*Crable pro pal*," which
was as much as to say that we had lost our ship.   And
many more words we could not use, because we understood not each other.   Then they made show to be
sorry for our loss, and to be grieved that we the year
before had been there with so many ships, and then
to see us in so simple manner, and made us signs that
then they had drunk wine in our ship, and asked us

what drink we had now. Wherewith one of our men went into the scute and drew some water, and let them taste thereof; but they shaked their heads, and said, "*No dobbre*," that is, "It is not good." Then our master went nearer unto them, and shewed them his mouth, to give them to understand that we were troubled with the scurvy, and to know if they could give us any counsel to help it. But they thought we made show that we had great hunger, wherewith one of them went unto their lodging and fetched a round rye loaf weighing about eight pounds, with some smoked fowls, which we accepted thankfully, and gave them in exchange half a dozen of biscuits. Then our master led two of the chief of them with him into his scute, and gave them some of the wine that we had, being about a quart, for it was so near out. And while we stayed there, we were very familiar with them, and went to the place where they lay, and sod some of our biscuit with water by their fire, that we might eat some warm thing down into our bodies. And we were much comforted to see the Russians, for that in thirteen months' time since that we departed from John Cornelison, we had not seen any man, but only monstrous and cruel wild bears; so that as then we were in some comfort, to see that we had lived so long, to come in company of men again. And therewith we said unto each other, "Now we hope that it will fall out better with us, seeing we have found men again," thanking God with all our hearts, that He had been so gracious and merciful unto us, to give us life until that time.

The 29 of July it was reasonable fair weather, and that morning the Russians began to make preparation to be gone and to set sail; at which time they digged certain barrels with train oil out of the shingle, which they had buried there, and put it into their ships. And we not knowing whither they would go, saw them sail towards the Weygats : at which time also we set sail and followed after them. But they sailing before us, and we following them along by the land, the weather being close and misty, we lost the sight of them.

The 31 of July we rowed to an island, and there, to our great good, we went on land, for in that island we found great store of leple leaves, which served us exceeding well; and it seemed that God had purposely sent us thither, for as then we had many sick men, and most of us were so troubled with the scurvy, and were thereby become so weak, that we could hardly row, but by means of those leaves we were healed thereof : for that as soon as we had eaten them, we were presently eased and healed; whereat we could not choose but wonder, and therefore we gave God great thanks for that and for many other His mercies showed unto us, by His great and unexpected aid, lent us in that our dangerous voyage. And so, as I said before, we ate them by whole handfuls together, because in Holland we had heard much spoken of their great force, and as then found it to be much more than we expected.

The 1 of August the wind blew hard north-west, and the ice, that for a while had driven towards the entry of the Weygats, stayed and drave no more, but the sea ran very high, whereby we were forced to remove our scutes on the other side of the island, to defend them from the waves of the sea. And lying there, we went on land again to fetch more leple leaves, whereby we had been so well holpen, and still more and more recovered our healths, and in so short time that we could not choose but wonder thereat; so that as then some of us could eat biscuit again, which not long before they could not do.

The 2 of August it was dark misty weather, the wind still blowing stiff north-west; at which time our victuals began to decrease, for as then we had nothing but a little bread and water, and some of us a little cheese; which made us long sore to be gone from thence, specially in regard of our hunger, whereby our weak members began to be much weaker; and yet we were forced to labour sore, which were two great contraries; for it behoved us rather to have our bellies full, that so we might be the stronger to endure our labour; but patience was our point of trust.

The 3 of August, about the north sun, the weather being somewhat better, we agreed amongst ourselves to leave Nova Zembla and to cross over to Russia.

The 4 of August we saw the coast of Russia lying before us, whereat we were exceeding glad.

The 5 of August, lying there, one of our men went on shore, and found the land further in to be green and full of trees, and from thence called to us to bid us bring our pieces on shore, saying that there was wild deer to be killed, which made us exceeding glad, for then our victuals were almost spent, and we had nothing but some broken bread, whereby we were wholly out of comfort, and some of us were of opinion that we should leave the scutes and go further into the land, or else (they said) we should all die with hunger, for that many days before we were forced to fast, and hunger was a sharp sword which we could hardly endure any longer.

The 6 of August the weather began to be somewhat better; at which time we determined to row forward, because the wind was against us, so that we might get out of the creek, the wind being east-south-east, which was our course as then. And so, having rowed about twelve miles, we could get no further, because it was so full in the wind, and we altogether heartless and faint, the land stretching further north-east than we made account it had done. Whereupon we beheld each other in pitiful manner, for we had great want of victuals, and knew not how far we had to sail, before we should get any relief; for all our victuals was almost consumed.

The 7 of August, the wind being west-north-west, it served us well to get out of that creek, and so we sailed forward east and by north till we got out of the creek, to the place and the point of land, where we first had been, and there made our scutes fast again; for the north-west wind was right against us, whereby our men's hearts and courages were wholly abated, to see no issue how we should get from thence; for as then sicknesses, hunger, and no means to be found how to get from thence, consumed both our flesh and our blood; but if we had found any relief, it would have been better with us.

The 8 of August there was no better weather, but still the wind was against us, and we lay a good way one from the other, as we found best place for us; at which time there was most sorrow in our boat, in regard that some of us were exceeding hungry, and could not endure it any longer, but were wholly out of heart, and wishing to die.

The 9 of August it was all one weather, so that,

the wind blowing contrary, we were forced to lie still and could go no further, our grief still increasing more and more. At last two of our men went out of the scute, wherein the master was; which we perceiving, two of our men also landed, and went all together about four miles into the country, and at last saw a beacon, by the which there issued a great stream of water, which we thought to be the way, from whence the Russians came between Candinaes and the firm land of Russia. And as our men came back again, in the way, as they went along, they found a dead seal, that stank exceedingly, which they drew with them to our boats, thinking that they should have a dainty morsel out of it, because they endured so great hunger; but we told them that without doubt it would kill us, and that it were better for us to endure poverty and hunger for a time, than to venture upon it; saying that, seeing God, who in so many great extremities had sent us a happy issue, still lived and was exceeding powerful, we hoped and nothing doubting that He would not altogether forsake us, but rather help us when we were most in despair.

The 10 of August it was still a north-west wind, with misty and dark weather, so that we were driven to lie still; at which time it was no need for us to ask one another how we fared, for we could well guess it by our countenances.

The 11 of August, in the morning, it was fair calm weather, so that, the sun being about north-east, the master sent one of his men to us, to bid us prepare ourselves to set sail, but we had made ourselves ready thereunto before he came, and began to row towards him. At which time, for that I was very weak and no longer able to row, as also for that our boat was harder to row than the scute, I was set in the scute to guide the helm, and one that was stronger was sent out of the scute into the boat to row in my place, that we might keep company together; and so we rowed till the sun was south, and then we had a good gale of wind out of the south, which made us take in our oars; and then we hoised up our sails, wherewith we made good way. But in the evening the wind began to blow hard, whereby we were forced to take in our sails and to row towards the land, where we laid our scutes close to the strand, and went on land to seek for fresh water, but found none. And because we could go no further, we laid our sails over the boats to cover us from the weather; at which time it began to rain very hard, and at midnight it thundered and lightened, with more store of rain, wherewith our company were much disquieted, to see that they found no means of relief, but still entered into further trouble and danger.

The 12 of August it was fair weather; at which time, the sun being east, we saw a Russian lodgie come towards us with all his sails up, wherewith we were not a little comforted, which we perceiving from the strand, where we lay with our scutes, we desired the master that we might go unto him to speak with him, and to get some victuals of them ; and to that end we made as much haste as we could to get the boats into deep water, and sailed towards them. And when we got to them, the master went into the lodgie to ask them how far we had to Candinaes, which we could not well learn of them, because we understood them not. They held up their five fingers unto us, but we knew not what they meant thereby; but after, we perceived that thereby they would show us, that there stood five crosses upon it; and they brought their compass out, and showed us, that it lay north-west from us, which our compass also showed us, which reckoning also we had made. But when we saw we could have no better intelligence from them, the master went further into their ship, and pointed to a barrel of fish that he saw therein, making signs to know whether they would sell it unto us, showing them a piece of eight reals. Which they understanding, gave us 102 fishes, with some cakes, which they had made of meal, when they sod their fish. And about the south sun we left them, being glad that we had gotten some victuals; for long before we had had but four ounces of bread a day with a little water, and nothing else, and with that we were forced to comfort ourselves as well as we could. The fishes we shared amongst us equally, to one as much as another, without any difference.

The 13 of August, sailing with a good wind, about midnight there rose a great storm out of the north, wherewith we stroke sail and made it shorter; but our other boat, that was harder under sail (knowing not that we had lessened our sails), sailed forward, whereby we strayed one from the other, for then it was very dark.

The 14 of August, in the morning, it being indifferent good weather with a south-west wind, we sailed west-north-west, and then it began to clear up, so that we saw our other boat, and did what we could to get unto her, but we could not, because it began to be misty weather again; and therefore we said unto each other, "Let us hold on our course: we shall find

them well enough on the north coast, when we are
past the White Sea."

The 15 of August we saw the sun rise east-north-
east, whereupon we thought that our compass varied
somewhat; and when the sun was east, it was calm
weather again, wherewith we were forced to take in
our sails and to row again, but it was not long before
we had a gale of wind out of the south-east, and then
we hoised up our sails again, and went forward west
and by south. And sailing in that manner with a
good forewind, when the sun was south we saw land,
thinking that as then we had been on the west side
of the White Sea beyond Candinaes; and being close
under the land, we saw six Russian lodgies lying there,
to whom we sailed and spake with them, asking them
how far we were from Kilduin. But although they
understood us not well, yet they made us such signs,
that we understood by them that we were still far from
thence, and that we were yet on the east side of Candinaes. And with that they stroke their hands together,
thereby signifying that we must first pass over the
White Sea, and that our scutes were too little to do it,
and that it would be over great danger for us to pass
over it with so small scutes, and that Candinaes was
still north-west from us. Then we asked them for
some bread, and they gave us a loaf, which we ate
hungerly up, as we were rowing; but we would not
believe them that we were still on the east side of
Candinaes, for we thought verily that we had passed
over the White Sea. And when we left them, we rowed
along by the land, the wind being north; and about
the north-west sun we had a good wind again from
the south-east, and therewith we sailed along by the

shore, and saw a great Russian lodgie lying on the starboard from us, which we thought came out of the White Sea.

The 16 of August, in the morning, sailing forward north-west, we perceived that we were in a creek, and so made towards the Russian lodgie, which we had seen on our starboard, which at last with great labour and much pain we got unto; and coming to them about the south-east sun, with a hard wind, we asked them how far we were from Zembla de Cool or Kilduin; but they shook their heads, and showed us that we were on the east side of Zembla de Candinaes, but we would not believe them. And then we asked them for some victuals, wherewith they gave us certain plaice, for the which the master gave them a piece of money; and we sailed from them again, to get out of that hole where we were, as it reached into the sea. But they perceiving that we took a wrong course, and that the flood was almost past, sent two men unto us, in a small boat, with a great loaf of bread, which they gave us, and made signs unto us to come back to their ship again, for that they intended to have further speech with us and to instruct us. Which we seemed not to refuse, and desiring not to be unthankful, gave them a piece of money and a piece of linen cloth; but they stayed still by us, and they that were in the great lodgie held up bacon and butter unto us, to move us to come aboard of them again, and so we did. And being with them, they showed us that we were still on the east side of the point of Candinaes. Then we fetched our card and let them see it, by the which they showed us that we were still on the east side of the White Sea and of Candinaes; which we understanding, were in some doubt with ourselves, because we had so great a voyage to make over the White Sea, and were in more fear for our companions that were in the boat, as also that having sailed 88 miles right across the sea, we had gotten no further, but were then to sail over the mouth of the White Sea with so small provision. For which cause the master bought of the Russians three sacks with meal, two flitches and a half of bacon, a pot of Russia butter, and a runlet of honey, for provision for us and our boat, when we should meet with it again. And for that in the meantime the flood was past, we sailed with the ebb out of the aforesaid creek, where the Russians' boat came to us, and entered into the sea with a good south-east wind, holding our course north-north-west; and there we saw a point that reached out into the sea, which we thought to be Candinaes, but we sailed still forward, and the land reached north-west. In the evening, the sun being north-west, when we saw that we did not much good with rowing, and that the stream was almost past, we lay still, and sod a pot full of water and meal, which tasted exceeding well, because we had put some bacon fat and honey into it, so that we thought it to be a festival day with us; but still our minds ran upon our boat, because we knew not where it was.

The 17 of August, lying at anchor, in the morning at break of day we saw a Russian lodgie, that came sailing out of the White Sea, to whom we rowed, that we might have some instruction from him; and when we boarded him, without asking or speaking unto him, he gave us a loaf of bread, and by signs showed us, as well as he could, that he had seen our companions, and that there was seven men in the boat. But we not knowing well what they said, neither yet believing them, they made other signs unto us, and held up their seven fingers and pointed to our scute, thereby showing that there were so many men in the boat, and that they had sold them bread, flesh, fish, and other victuals. And while we stayed in their lodgie, we saw a small compass therein, which we knew that they had bought of our chief boatswain, which they likewise acknowledged. Then we understanding them well, asked them how long it was since they saw our boat, and whereabouts it was, and they made signs unto us, that it was the day before. And to conclude, they showed us great friendship, for the which we thanked them; and so, being glad of the good news we had heard, we took our leaves of them, much rejoicing that we heard of our companions' welfare, and specially because they had gotten victuals from the Russians, which was the thing that we most doubted of, in regard that we knew what small provision they had with them. Which done, we rowed as hard as we could, to try if we might overtake them, as being still in doubt that they had not provision enough, wishing that they had had part of ours: and having rowed all that day with great labour along by the land, about midnight we found a fall of fresh water, and then we went on land to fetch some, and there also we got some leple leaves. And as we thought to row forward, we were forced to sail, because the flood was past, and still we looked earnestly out for the point of Candinaes, and the five crosses, whereof we had been instructed by the Russians, but we could not see it.

The 18 of August, in the morning, the sun being

east, we pulled up our stone (which we used instead
of an anchor), and rowed along by the land till the
sun was south. Then we saw a point of land reaching
into the sea, and on it certain signs of crosses, which,
as we went nearer unto, we saw perfectly; and when the
sun was west, we perceived that the land reached west
and south-west, so that thereby we knew it certainly
to be the point of Candinaes, lying at the mouth of
the White Sea, which we were to cross, and had long
desired to see it.

And so, having a good north-east wind (which it
would not do for us to neglect), we set forward in the
name of God, and we took our departure when the sun
was north-west, and all that night and the next day
sailed with a good wind, and in all that time rowed but
while three glasses were run out; and the next night
after ensuing, having still a good wind, in the morning
about the east-north-east sun we saw land on the west
side of the White Sea, which we found by the rushing of
the sea upon the land before we saw it. And perceiving
it to be full of cliffs, and not low sandy ground with
some hills, as it is on the east side of the White Sea, we
assured ourselves that we were on the west side of the
White Sea, upon the coast of Lapland; for the which
we thanked God, that He had helped us to sail over
the White Sea in thirty hours, it being 160 miles at
the least, our course being west with a north-east
wind.

The 20 of August, being not far from the land,
the north-east wind left us, and then it began to blow
stiff north-west; at which time, seeing we could not
make much way by sailing forward, we determined
to put in between certain cliffs, and when we got close

to the land we espied certain crosses with directions upon them, whereby we understood that it was a good roadstead, and so put into it. And being entered a little way within it, we saw a great Russian lodgie lying at an anchor, whereunto we rowed as fast as we could, and there also we saw certain houses wherein men dwelt. And when we got to the lodgie, we anchored there, and cast our tent over the scute, for as then it began to rain. Then we went on land into the houses that stood upon the shore, where they showed us great friendship, leading us into their stoves, and there dried our wet clothes, and then, seething some fish, bade us sit down and eat somewhat with them. In those little houses we found thirteen Russians, who every morning went out to fish in the sea; whereof two of them had charge over the rest. They lived very poorly, and ordinarily ate nothing but fish. At evening, when we prepared ourselves to go to our scute again, they prayed the master and me to stay with them in their houses, which the master thanked them for, would not do, but I stayed with them all that night.

The 21 of August, after noon, we saw two men upon the hills, whereupon we said one to the other, " Hereabouts there must more people dwell, for there come two men towards us "; but we, regarding them not, went back again to our scute and towards the houses. The two men that were upon the hills (being some of our men that were in the other boat), perceiving also the Russian lodgie, came down the hill towards her to buy some victuals of them. Who being come thither unprepared and having no money about them, they agreed between them to put off one of their pair of breeches (for that as then we wore two or three pair, one over the other), to sell them for some victuals.   But when they came down the hill and were somewhat nearer unto us, they espied our scute lying by the lodgie, and we as then beheld them better and knew them; wherewith we rejoiced, and showed each other of our proceedings, and how we had sailed to and fro in great necessity and hunger, and yet they had been in greater necessity and danger, than we, and gave God thanks that He had preserved us alive, and brought us together again.   And then we ate something together, and drank of the clear water, such as runneth along by Cologne through the Rhine, and then we agreed that they should come unto us, that we might sail together.

The 22 of August the rest of our men with the boat came unto us about the east-south-east sun, whereat we much rejoiced, and then we prayed the Russians' cook to bake a sack of meal for us, and to make it bread, paying him for it, which he did.   And in the meantime, when the fishermen came with their fish out of the sea, our master bought four cods of them, which we sod and ate.   And while we were at meat, the chief of the Russians came unto us, and perceiving that we had not much bread, he fetched a loaf and gave it us, and although we desired them to sit down and eat some meat with us, yet we could by no means get them to grant thereunto, because it was their fasting day, and for that we had poured butter and fat into our fish; nor we could not get them once to drink with us, because our cup was somewhat greasy, they were so superstitious touching their fasting and religion.   Neither would they lend us any of their cups to drink in, lest they should likewise be greased. At that time the wind was constantly north-west.

The 23 of August the cook began to knead our meal, and made us bread thereof. Which being done, and the wind and the weather beginning to be somewhat better, we made ourselves ready to depart from thence; at which time, when the Russians came from fishing, our master gave their chief commander a good piece of money, in regard of the friendship that he had showed us, and gave somewhat also to the cook, for the which they yielded us great thanks. At which time, the chief of the Russians desired our master to give him some gunpowder, which he did. And when we were ready to sail from thence, we put a sack of meal out of our scute into the boat, lest we should chance to stray one from the other again, that they might help themselves therewith. And so about evening, when the sun was west, we set sail and departed from thence, and on the 25 we got to the west end of Kilduin.

And when we came there, we found a small house upon the shore, wherein there was three men and a great dog, which received us very friendly, asking us of our affairs and how we got thither. Whereunto we made answer, and showed them that we had lost our ship, and that we were come thither, to see if we could get a ship, that would bring us into Holland. Whereunto they made us answer, that there was three ships at Kola, whereof two were to set sail from thence that day. Then we asked them, if they would go with one of our men by land to Kola, to look for a ship wherewith we might get into Holland, and said we would reward them well for their pains; but they excused themselves, and said that they could not go from thence, but they said that they would bring us over the hill, where we should find certain Laplanders, whom they thought would go with us, as they did; for the master and one of our men going with them over the hill, found certain Laplanders there, whereof they got one to go with our man, promising him two reals of eight for his pains.

The 29 of August it was indifferent fair weather, and we were still in good hope to hear some good news from Kola, and always looked up towards the hill, to see if our man and the Laplander came; but seeing they came not, we went to the Russians again, and there drest our meat, and then meant to go to our scutes to lodge in them all night. In the meantime we spied the Laplander coming alone without our man, whereat we wondered and were somewhat in doubt; but when he came unto us, he showed us a letter, that was written unto our master, which he opened before us, the contents thereof being that he, that had written the letter, wondered much at our arrival in that place, and that long since he verily thought that we had been all cast away, being exceeding glad of our happy fortune, and how that he would presently come unto us with victuals, and all other necessaries to succour us withal. We being in no small admiration, who it might be, that showed us so great favour and friendship, could not imagine what he was, for it appeared by the letter that he knew us well. And although the letter was subscribed "by me, John Cornelison Rijp," yet we could not be persuaded that it was the same John Cornelison, who the year before had been set out in the other ship with us, and left us about the Bear Island. For those good news we paid the Laplander his hire, and beside that, gave him hose, breeches, and other furniture, so that he was apparelled like a Hollander; for as then we thought ourselves to be wholly out of danger, and so being of good comfort, we laid us down to rest. Here I cannot choose but show you how fast the Laplander went: for when he went to Kola, as our companion told us, they were two days and two nights on the way, and yet went apace; and when he came back again, he was but a day and a night coming to us, which was wonderful, it being but half the time, so that we said, and verily thought, that he was half a conjurer; and he brought us a partridge, which he had killed by the way, as he went.

The 30 of August it was indifferent fair weather, we still wondering, who that John Cornelison might be, that had written unto us; and while we sat musing thereon, some of us were of opinion, that it might be the same John Cornelison, that had sailed out of Holland in company with us; which we could not be persuaded to believe, because we were in as little hope of his life, as he of ours, supposing that he had sped worse than we, and long before that had been cast away. At last the master said, "I will look amongst my letters, for there I have his handwriting, and that will put us out of doubt." And so, looking amongst them, we found that it was the same John Cornelison; wherewith we were as glad of his safety and welfare, as he was of ours. And while we were speaking thereof, and that some of us would not believe that it was the same John Cornelison, we saw a Russian joll come rowing, with John Cornelison and our companion, that we

13—2

had sent to Kola. Who being landed, we received and welcomed each other with great joy and exceeding gladness, as if either of us on both sides had seen each other rise from death to life again; for we esteemed him, and he us, to be dead long since. He brought us a barrel of Roswick beer, wine, aqua vitae, bread, flesh, bacon, salmon, sugar, and other things, which comforted and relieved us much. And we rejoiced together for our so unexpected meeting, at that time giving God great thanks for His mercy showed unto us.

The 31 of August it was indifferent fair weather, the wind easterly, but in the evening it began to blow hard from the land; and then we made preparation to sail from thence to Kola, first taking our leaves of the Russians, and heartily thanking them for their courtesy showed unto us, and gave them a piece of money for their good wills; and at night, about the north sun, we sailed from thence at high water.

The 1 of September, in the morning, with the east sun, we got to the west side of the river of Kola.

The 11 of September, by leave and consent of the boyard, governor for the Great Prince of Muscovia, we brought our scute and our boat into the merchants' house, and there let them stand for a remembrance of our long, far, and never before sailed way, and that we had sailed in those open scutes almost 1600 miles, through and along by the sea coasts to the town of Kola, whereat the inhabitants thereof could not sufficiently wonder.

The 15 of September we went into a lodgie, and sailed down the river with all our goods and our men to John Cornelison's ship, which lay about two miles from the town, and that day sailed in the ship down the river, till we were beyond the narrowest part thereof, which was about half the river, and there stayed for John Cornelison and our master, that said they would come to us the next day.

The 17 of September, John Cornelison and our master being come aboard, the next day, about the east sun, we set sail out of the river of Kola, and with God's grace put to sea to sail homewards; and upon the first of November, about noon, got to Amsterdam, in the same clothes that we ware in Nova Zembla, with our caps furred with white foxes' skins, and went to the house of Peter Hasselaer, that was one of the merchants that set out the two ships, which were conducted by John Cornelison and our master. And being there, where many men wondered to see us, as having esteemed us long before that to have been dead and rotten, the news thereof being spread abroad in the town, it was also carried to the Prince's Court in the Hague; at which time the Lord Chancellor of Denmark, ambassador for the said king, was then at dinner with Prince Maurice. For the which cause we were presently fetched thither by the scout and two of the burghers of the town, and there, in the presence of the said lord ambassador and the burgomasters, we made rehearsal of our journey both forwards and backwards. And after that, every man that dwelt thereabouts went home, but such as dwelt not near to that place, were placed in good lodgings for certain days, until we had received our pay, and then every one of us departed and went to the place of his abode.

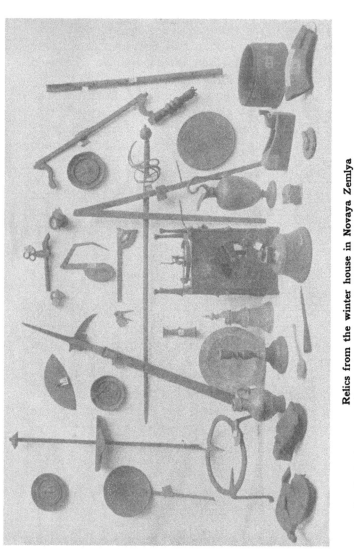

Relics from the winter house in Novaya Zemlya

In the Nederlandsch Museum voor Geschiedenis en Kunst (National Museum), Amsterdam.

APPENDIX TO THE THIRD VOYAGE
OF W. BARENTS

Although Dutch walrus-hunters and others had been near the house where Barents and his companions wintered, the spot was unvisited for nearly 300 years. In 1871 a Norwegian sloop, *The Solid*, Captain Carlsen, reached the coast of Novaya Zemlya. The following are extracts from his log :

"Saturday, Sep. 9 . . . . . 6 o'clock in the afternoon, we saw walrus on the ice, boats were lowered, and we caught two of them; we also saw a house on shore, which had fallen down. At noon we observed the latitude 76° 12′, the distance from shore guessed. The house on shore was 16 metres long by 10 metres broad, and the fir-wood planks, of which it was composed, were 1½ inches thick by from 14 to 16 inches broad, and as far as we could make out they were nailed together. The first things we saw amongst the ruins of the house were two ships' cooking pans of copper, a crowbar or bar of iron, a gun-barrel, an alarum, a clock, a chest in which was found several files and other instruments, many engravings, a flute, and also a few articles of dress. There were also two other chests, but they were empty, only filled up with ice, and there was an iron frame over the fireplace with shifting bar.

"Tuesday, 12. Gale from the S.W. We are obliged to return to Ledenaji Bay (Ice Harbour), where on the evening of the 9th we had found the ruined house. At noon we anchored in the bay, and went again on shore and found several things, viz.: candle-sticks, tankards with lid of zinc, a sword, a halberd head, two books, several navigation instruments, an iron chest already quite rusted.

"Thursday, 14. Calm with clear sky. 4 o'clock in the morning we went ashore further to investigate the wintering place. On digging we found again several objects, such as drumsticks, a hilt of a sword, and spears. Altogether it seemed that the people had been equipped in a warlike manner, but nothing was found which could indicate the presence of human remains. On the beach we found pieces of wood which had formerly belonged to some part of a ship, for which reason I believe that a vessel has been wrecked there, the crew of which built the house with the materials of the wreck and afterwards betook themselves to the boats. Five sailors' trunks were still in the house, which might also have been used as five berths, at least as far as we could make out."

On his return, a Norwegian newspaper published an article containing a few further details, which were supplied probably by Carlsen himself. He had found the house "almost hermetically enclosed by a thick layer of ice. All the objects were likewise covered by a thick sheet of ice, and this explains the excellent condition, in which many of the articles were found." Among them were "a few books in the Dutch language, which latter makes it almost certain that the relics belonged to Barendsz and his companions of the year 1596. In the centre of the house, where the fireplace had probably stood, a great iron frame was found, on which two ship's copper cooking pans still remained."

Probably some of these things (e.g. the engravings) were merchandise—intended for China—of which the ship's cargo partly consisted. In 1875 another Norwegian, Gundersen, visited Ice Harbour and found in a chest a manuscript Dutch translation of Pet and Jackman's Voyage of 1580, two charts, etc.

Lastly in 1876, an Englishman, Mr Charles Gardiner, in the yacht *Glow-worm*, landed and spent three days in searching the ruined house, and discovered more than a hundred articles under the ice. These consisted largely of remains of carpenters' tools, weapons, and sailors' materials. There were also a seal, a lead inkstand, quill pens, an iron pair of compasses, a harpoon, twenty wax candles, three Dutch books, two Dutch coins, a measure, and the ship's flag of Amsterdam. In one of the powder-horns was the manuscript which Barents left behind hung up in the chimney —a short record signed by Barents and Heemskerck— legible except for a few words.

These relics are now in the National Museum at Amsterdam.

NOTES

FROBISHER: FIRST VOYAGE

The black figures refer to pages and the plain figures to lines.

1, 1. General. The commander of a fleet. His ship was the Admiral.

2. **Cataya** (or Cathay). Another name for China. Knowledge was so vague that these were sometimes thought to be distinct empires.

Capo de Buona Sperança. The Cape of Good Hope.

2, 26. pretended. Intended.

29. **He departed upon the said voyage from Blackwall.** On the way down the Thames they passed the Court, then at Greenwich, "where we shot off our ordnance and made the best show we could. Her Majesty, beholding the same, commended it, and bade us farewell, with shaking her hand at us out of the window." (From the account of the voyage by Hall, Master in the *Gabriel.*)

4, 3. Frisland. An imaginary land on old charts near the east coast of Greenland. Frobisher had really reached South Greenland.

5, 15. Frobisher's Straits. The bay (Frobisher Bay) in the south of Baffin Land, to the north of Hudson Strait.

24. **mankind.** Masculine, vicious. "A mankind witch." Shakespeare, *Winter's Tale*, II. iii.

6, 27. come within our men's danger. Get into their power.

33. **lowbell.** A bell used in bird-batting (a method of taking birds at night with a net and light).

8, 24. marquesite. From an Arab word meaning pyrites. This mineral sometimes contains a trace of gold.

26. **goldfiners.** Gold refiners or assayers.

FROBISHER: SECOND VOYAGE

10, 3. **Cataya, China.** See note p. 1, l. 2.

11, 36. **Hope.** An anchorage.

12, 10. **condemned men.** Criminals who were to be landed in Greenland with food and weapons.

19. **[cipher] leagues.** To keep the course secret, distances, etc., were in cipher in the manuscript.

13, 17. **durance.** Imprisonment.

14, 9. **account.** Reckoning.

19. **Frisland.** See note p. 4, l. 3.

15, 1. **Zeni.** The accounts of these voyages in the 14th century were probably a 16th century forgery, with the object of proving that the Venetians had discovered America a century before Columbus.

4. **sithence.** Since.

5. **sea-cards.** Charts.

16, 1. **bearing yet the dominion.** Keeping still above it.

11. **surcease.** Cease.

17, 8. **Hall's Island.** Cape Enderby (at the northern entrance of Frobisher Bay).

19, 11. **wafting.** Beckoning.
        " In such a night
    Stood Dido with a willow in her hand
    Upon the wild sea banks, and waft her love
    To come again to Carthage."
            Shakespeare, *Merchant of Venice*, v. i.

24. **point.** A lace with a tag used for fastening articles of dress.

21, 12. **caliver.** A large pistol or blunderbuss.

16. **furniture.** Armour.

23, 16. **marquesite.** See note p. 8, l. 24.

28. **say.** Assay.

31. **a great dead fish.** A narwhal.

25, 16. **northland.** Supposed to be part of Asia. See p. 5, l. 12.

28, 4. **cony bury.** A rabbit's burrow.

29, 12. **advisedly.** With deliberation.

14. **whether.** Which of the two.

15. **lively.** Living.

33, 4. **let.** Hindered.

sea room. Clear space for allowing a ship to turn, etc.

"Give us but a good ship and sea room, and we think nothing of such a squall of wind as that."

Robinson Crusoe (Golden Treasury Edition, p. 7).

35, 9. **Queen's Cape.** Cape Resolution in Resolution Island off the southern entrance of Frobisher Bay.

36, 24. **kindness.** Natural disposition.

39, 11. **mine.** Mineral ore.

42, 1. **for fashion sake.** For the sake of custom, or courtesy.

2. **cater.** Caterer, one who provides food.

18. **spoil.** Plunder. Compare "to spoil the Egyptians."

43, 1. **belayed.** Lain hidden.

46, 5. **branded.** A mixture of red and black.

9. **board.** Tack.

31. **Bristow.** Bristol.

DAVIS: FIRST VOYAGE

49, 20. **harping iron.** Harpoon.

50, 12. **breach.** Where the waves break.

21. **glass.** A sand-glass running out in half-an-hour (used until recently in the Royal Navy).

30. **falconet.** A light cannon.

51, 3. **along the coast.** The east coast of Greenland, north of Cape Farewell.

9. **list.** The torn edge of cloth. Here "torn cloud."

13. **Land of Desolation.** Considered a new discovery, distinct from the land seen by Frobisher (which he supposed to be Frisland). Longitudes are not given in Frobisher's Voyages, and Davis made Frobisher's Strait pass through Greenland, with an island to the south. So it appears on the New Map of the World, published about 1600.

53, 5. **sounds.** Here was Gilbert Sound (64° 8′ N.), now Godthaab, a Danish settlement.

56, 3. **scull.** School or shoal.

7. **Meta Incognita.** The Unknown Bourne. Queen Elizabeth gave this name to the land bordering Frobisher Bay on the south (South-east Baffin Land).

8. **Muscovy glass.** Mica, which was used in parts of Russia instead of glass.

11. **corinth.** Now altered to "currant." Named after the town of Corinth, and given originally to the small dried grapes which came from the Levant.

14. **present.** Present month.

57, 2. **Cape Walsingham.** They had crossed the strait and reached Baffin Land, north of Cumberland Sound.

58, 6. **bravest.** Brave commonly meant "finely dressed."

16. **Newland.** Newfoundland.

20. **Cape of God's Mercy.** At the north entrance of Cumberland Sound.

25. **entrance or passage.** Cumberland Sound.

59, 30. **flean.** Flayed.

61, 10. **snite.** A snipe, so called from the length of the bill or *snout.*

24. **tried.** "To try" is to lie under try-sails (i.e. with very little sail set).

25. **goose wing.** A sail with only its lower corners set.

DAVIS: SECOND VOYAGE

62, 10. **land.** The southern extremity of Greenland. Here Davis divided his fleet, and sent the *Sunshine* and *Northstar* to seek a passage northward between Greenland and Iceland. After harbouring in Iceland, they sailed north-west, reached "two firm lands of ice," and then turned back towards Greenland and reached Gilbert Sound on August 3rd. Failing to meet the rest of the fleet here, as arranged, they left for England on August 31st. On September 3rd, in a very great storm, the *Sunshine* lost sight of the *Northstar* and reached England alone at the end of the month.

63, 4. **same place.** Gilbert Sound. There is an error in Davis's longitude.

64, 16. **salmon peel.** Young salmon weighing less than 2 lbs.

29. **train oil.** An oil got from the whale.

65, 11. **gripe.** (Griffin) Gerfalcon.

66, 10. **Iliaout.** "I mean no harm." So interpreted by the explorers.

14. **elan.** Elk.

17. **witches.** Used for the masculine (wizards).

25. **train.** See note p. 64, l. 29.

67, 12. **caliver.** See note to Frobisher 2, p. 21, l. 12.

18. **falcon.** A cannon larger than a falconet, about 7 feet in length, throwing a 3 lb. ball.

68, 7. **artificially.** Skilfully.

69, 9. **to stop a flood.** To wait for the flood tide (which was against them) to ebb.

10. **miscreants.** Unbelievers.

26. **tolled.** Drew, enticed.

71, 30. **stickle.** Rapid.

72, 25. **contentation.** Content.

73, 7. **the land in latitude 66 degrees, etc.** The American shore of the strait.

13. **graved the Moonshine.** "To grave" is to clean a ship's bottom of weeds, etc., and tar it.

22. **flood.** The flood tide.

74, 19. **a very fair promontory.** The Cape of God's Mercy, which he had discovered and named on his first voyage.

75, 3. **to lie at hull.** To lie-to, i.e. to come almost to a stop with head near wind. "To hull" also means to drive without sails or rudder.

9. **a very high hill.** Probably on Resolution Island, at the entrance of Hudson Strait.

21. **lay upon the lee.** Heaved-to.

76, 1. **pheasant, partridge.** Ptarmigans.

8. **coasted the shore.** Labrador.

16. **suavle.** Possibly a corruption of sweþel, close packed.

17. **scull.** See note p. 56, l. 3.

24. **two lands west.** Hamilton Inlet (Labrador), or the strait between Newfoundland and the mainland.

77, 13. **presently.** At the present, at once.

27. **junk.** An old, worn out rope.

DAVIS: THIRD VOYAGE

78, 9. **clincher.** A clinker-built pinnace (made with the outside planks overlapping one another). Two of the ships were to go fishing, to help pay expenses.

79, 28. **we discovered land.** The west coast of Greenland. The south coast had been rounded without being seen.

80, 8. **kerned.** Corned, granulated.

20. **saker.** An old kind of cannon, eight to ten feet long, throwing a 4 lb. to 7 lb. shot.

81, 17. **had three hundred strokes.** To keep the water out of the ship, three hundred strokes of the pump were necessary during one watch (four hours).

82, 12. **unicorn.** See Frobisher 2, p. 24, l. 5.

28. **chichsanege.** Probably sealskins.

83, 4. **London Coast.** Greenland.

8. **Hope Sanderson.** After the London merchant to whom the enterprise owed so much (see p. 48, l. 20). This was the extreme northern point reached.

shaped our course west. Crossing the gulf now called Baffin Bay.

84, 14. **we were thwart the straits.** The ice had forced them southwards, so that land was not seen until they were about the narrow part of Davis Strait.

27. **hot.** "This 25 we were becalmed almost in the bottom of the straits, and had the weather marvellous extreme hot "— Davis's Log-book.

85, 7. **ruts.** The dashing of waves.

20. **a very great gulf.** Hudson Strait.

26. **Chidley's Cape.** Named after John Chudleigh or Chidley, an intimate friend of Davis.

87, 1. **Biscayan.** The Biscayans were expert whale fishers, and from them the English learnt the art. In early times a species of large whale frequented the Bay of Biscay and the Atlantic, and was the most important source of wealth to the ports from St Jean de Luz to Santander. This gradually disappeared, and the Basque fishermen sailed north for whales to Newfoundland and Spitzbergen. When the English began to fish for whales round Spitzbergen, they used to enter a number of these men in each fleet.

HUDSON : LAST VOYAGE

89, 6. **the capes where the fowl bred.** Cape Wolstenholme and one opposite on Digges Islands. They were named by Hudson after two of the principal merchants responsible for the voyage— Sir Dudley Digges and Sir John Wolstenholme.

91, 18. **piece.** A gun.

94, 19. **seine.** A fishing net.

97, 3. **they would have me stay in the ship.** The mutineers had saved Prickett, " as is thought, in hope by Sir Dudley Digges, his master, to procure their pardon at their return."

100, 12. **He rose and went into the hold.** i.e. John King.

101, 8. **horn.** A thin plate of horn, serving as a window.

12. **the carpenter.** Philip Staffe, an Ipswich man.

27. **the capes.** See p. 89, l. 6, and note.

102, 16. **John Hudson.** Henry Hudson's son, according to Purchas.

103, 23. **card.** Chart.

28. tale. Number.

105, 17. **the capes.** They had lost their way, and were longing to reach the Capes (Wolstenholme and Digges), where they had entered Hudson Bay, and where they had found a plentiful supply of birds.

107, 29. **a snare.** A slip-knot.

108, 5. **morses.** Walruses.

109, 16. **Jews' trumps.** Jew's-harps.

111, 29. **it feared.** Frightened.

our master. Bylot.

112, 12. **lay a-try.** See note p. 61, l. 24.

28. the Desolations. South Greenland.

113, 13. **reasty.** Generally of bacon: rancid.

29. steep-tub. A large tub for soaking salt provisions before cooking.

114, 6. **the Durseys.** Dursey Island, off the west coast of Ireland, to the north of the entrance to Bantry Bay.

12. Bere Haven. In Bantry Bay.

20. Sir Thomas Smith. One of the principal merchants responsible for the voyage.

BARENTS: THIRD VOYAGE

116, 10. **Barents.** Barentsz, a contraction of Barentszoon (which was his proper name), meaning son of Barent or Bernard.

26. cross through the great roundel. Right through the great circle (of the former rainbow).

117, 11. **island.** Bear Island, sometimes called Cherry Island.

118, 9. **four glasses.** Two hours.

18. brooked it not well. It did not agree with us.

22. we saw land again. Spitzbergen (though they supposed it to be part of Greenland).

120, 2. **scute.** Any small boat. The smaller boat (the yawl) is sometimes referred to by the translator as "the boat": sometimes both are called "scutes."

121, 12. **brent geese.** Called also "barnacle" geese. They are smaller than a goose, with black and white feathers.

27. burst in sunder and are lost. A fable which commonly believed in the 16th century until this account was published.

123, 8. **Ice Point.** The northernmost point of Novaya Zemlya.

127, 33. **vice.** A screw or jack.

128, 29. **harts and hinds.** " Deer and elks."

129, 4. **wound.** Tacked.

130, 30. **with more ease.** " Three remained behind with the wood, to hew it, so that it might be the lighter to draw."

131, 1. **the principals.** The beams or principal timbers.

6. **to make up our house.** " To close up (the sides) of the house."

132, 22. **overhead.** " Somewhat higher in the middle."

133, 10. **cabins.** Cots.

17. **shot at her with pieces of wood.** " Threw pieces of fire-wood at her."

29. **spruce-beer.** Originally a decoction in beer or water of the leaf-buds of the spruce fir, used for rheumatism, etc. After-wards applied to beer brewed at Dantzic, without these leaf-buds.

135, 13. **no means to shoot.** Their firearms had matchlocks.

31. **strike.** " We set up our clock, so that it (went and) struck (the hour)."

136, 10. **chirurgeon.** Surgeon (who was also the barber).

15, 16. **at the setting of the sun....it rose.** When the sun disappeared and when it came back again.

23. **in the highest degree.** At 76° the moon continues above the horizon for 7 or 8 days every month.

139, 23. **sea-coals.** " Stone or mineral coal " : so called to distinguish it from charcoal, the usual fuel on the continent. *Sea-coal* was applied originally to coal brought by sea from Newcastle.

142, 26. **disease.** Discomfort.

143, 8. **Twelfth Even.** " Three Kings' Even." Twelfth-night is really on January 5th—the eve of the festival of Epiphany —but since the Reformation it has been kept on January 6th.

145, 11. **broke our fasts.** " Ate the funeral meal."

149, 27. **the stairs.** The steps cut in the snow.

151, 13. **in the highest.** A mistake for " lowest." He meant that the sun was on the meridian in the north.

154, 10. **arquebus.** An early kind of portable gun, supported on a rest, or by a hook on a tripod.

155, 14. **a piece of a buck, etc.** " Pieces of seals with the skin and hair."

25. **to amend our boat withal.** " Wherewith to raise the gunwale of our yawl."

160, 1. **into a musket's charge.** "And William Barents had previously written a small scroll and placed it in a *bandoleer*."

33. **dryfats.** Trunks.

162, 22. **.Ice Point.** See note p. 123, l. 8.

163, 30. **howell.** Hummock.

168, 18. **to discharge.** To empty and re-load.

170, 1. **impeachments.** Hindrances.

7. **mended.** "Where we had added to it."

31. **dryfat.** See note p. 160, l. 33.

33. **bunged with the ice.** Was stove in by the ice.

171, 28. **helm stick.** The tiller of the rudder.

173, 26. **eight foot thick.** Eight feet in girth.

176, 14. **between every meal-tide.** In every 24 hours.

26. **the Black Point.** Cape Negro.

178, 11. **had been in our ship.** During the previous voyage.

179, 10. **lodging.** Like lodgie (p. 177, l. 8), intended for a Russian word for boat.

22. **departed from John Cornelison.** At Bear Island, on July 1st, 1596. See p. 122.

180, 33. **leple leaves.** Scurvy grass.

181, 16. **point of trust.** "Patience was our fore-land," namely, always before them.

182, 4. **get out of the creek.** The mouth of the river Petchora.

24. **if we had found any relief.** "If looking deplorable could have helped us."

183, 9. **Candinaes.** Cape Kanin Nos, at the entrance to the White Sea.

21. **when we were most in despair.** "But help us when least foreseen."

184, 21. **Russian lodgie.** See note p. 179, l. 10.

185, 9. **a piece of eight reals.** A Spanish dollar. A real was a silver coin worth about sixpence.

186, 1. **the north coast.** "The coast of Norway."

11. **we saw land.** The west side of Tcheskaia Bay.

16. **Kilduin.** Kildin Island, off the coast of Lapland.

187, 10. **Zembla de Cool.** Zemlya is the Russian word for land. Cool is Kola in Lapland.

188, 20. **Stream.** Tide.

189, 9. **chief boatswain.** The first mate.

28. **And as we thought to row forward, we were forced to sail, because the flood was past.** "When we intended to proceed on our voyage, we were forced to remain lying there, because the tide had run out."

190, 16. **three glasses were run out.** An hour and a half.

191, 11. **stoves.** Rooms heated by a stove.

192, 12. **drank of the clear water.** "Drank of the pure article." There is a play on the Dutch word for "clear" or "pure," which is applied to spirits as well as to water.

194, 7. **two reals of eight.** Two Spanish dollars of eight reals. See note p. 185, l. 9.

195, 1. **about the Bear Island.** See p. 122.

3. **furniture.** Anything that furnishes. Often "armour"; here "clothes."

32. **joll.** A yawl.

196, 6. **Roswick.** A town in West Bothnia (Sweden).

aqua vitae. Here used for gin.

20. **the river of Kola.** The entrance to Kola is a bay, not a river.

22. **boyard.** A Russian title for a nobleman, or great man.

197, 21. **Prince Maurice.** A mistranslation. There is nothing about the Hague or Prince Maurice in the original, which runs: " where the noble lords, the Chancellor and the Ambassador from the most illustrious King of Denmark, Norway, Goths and Vandals, were then at table."

22. **the scout and two of the burghers of the town.** The sheriff and two town-councillors.

29. **every one of us departed, etc.** Twelve men (out of the original ship's company of seventeen) returned.

9 781107 600614